Decoding the TOEFL® iBT

Intermediate

WRITING

INTRODUCTION

For many learners of English, the TOEFL® iBT will be the most important standardized test they ever take. Unfortunately for a large number of these individuals, the material covered on the TOEFL® iBT remains a mystery to them, so they are unable to do well on the test. We hope that by using the *Decoding the TOEFL® iBT* series, individuals who take the TOEFL® iBT will be able to excel on the test and, in the process of using the book, may unravel the mysteries of the test and therefore make the material covered on the TOEFL® iBT more familiar to themselves.

The TOEFL® iBT covers the four main skills that a person must learn when studying any foreign language: reading, listening, speaking, and writing. The *Decoding the TOEFL® iBT* series contains books that cover all four of these skills. The *Decoding the TOEFL® iBT* series contains books with three separate levels for all four of the topics as well as the *Decoding the TOEFL® iBT Actual Test* books. These books are all designed to enable learners to utilize them to become better prepared to take the TOEFL® iBT. This book, *Decoding the TOEFL® iBT Writing Intermediate*, covers the writing aspect of the test. It is designed to help learners prepare for the Writing section of the TOEFL® iBT.

Decoding the TOEFL® iBT Writing Intermediate can be used by learners who are taking classes and also by individuals who are studying by themselves. It contains two parts, each of which contains ten chapters. Part A covers the Integrated Writing Task while Part B covers the Independent Writing Task. There is also one actual test at the end of the book. Each chapter has either two Integrated tasks or two Independent questions. It also contains exercises designed to help learners understand how to write the best possible essays for the Writing section. The passages and questions in *Decoding the TOEFL® iBT Writing Intermediate* are slightly lower levels than those found on the TOEFL® iBT. Individuals who use *Decoding the TOEFL® iBT Writing Intermediate* will therefore be able to prepare themselves not only to take the TOEFL® iBT but also to perform well on the test.

We hope that everyone who uses *Decoding the TOEFL® iBT Writing Intermediate* will be able to become more familiar with the TOEFL® iBT and will additionally improve his or her score on the test. As the title of the book implies, we hope that learners can use it to crack the code on the TOEFL® iBT, to make the test itself less mysterious and confusing, and to get the highest grade possible. Finally, we hope that both learners and instructors can use this book to its full potential. We wish all of you the best of luck as you study English and prepare for the TOEFL® iBT, and we hope that *Decoding the TOEFL® iBT Writing Intermediate* can provide you with assistance during the course of your studies.

Michael A. Putlack
Stephen Poirier

TABLE
OF
CONTENTS

Part A Integrated Writing Task

Part B Independent Writing Task

ABOUT THE TOEFL® iBT WRITING SECTION

How the Section Is Organized

The writing section is the last part of the TOEFL® iBT and consists of two portions: the Integrated Writing Task and the Independent Writing Task. The Integrated Writing Task requires test takers to explain how a short reading passage and lecture are related while the Independent Writing Task requires test takers to explain their opinions about a given situation. Test takers have 20 minutes to complete the Integrated Writing Task. For the Independent Writing Task, they have 30 minutes.

The writing section tests the ability of test takers to organize information clearly. The responses do not have to be creative or original. They just need to be succinct and direct. The most important thing test takers can do to boost their score is to present their ideas clearly by using relevant examples. Strong support and vivid details are essential for earning a top score.

Changes in the Writing Section

There are no major changes in the Writing section. However, in the Independent Writing Task, the directions tend to be longer than before on average. The question also often asks not only about a general opinion but also about a specific situation. This can be seen as a measure to prevent test takers from writing memorized essays. At the end of the question, there are directions that prohibit the writing of a memorized example. Therefore, it is important that test takers practice writing essays based on their own ideas instead of trying to memorize model essays.

Question Types

TYPE 1 The Integrated Writing Task

The Integrated Writing Task consists of three parts. Test takers begin by reading a passage approximately 230 to 300 words in length for 3 minutes. Following this, test takers listen to a lecture that either supports or contradicts the reading. Finally, test takers are given 20 minutes to write their essays. The essays should be between 150 and 225 words in length. During this time, the reading passage will reappear on the computer screen. Again, it is important to remember that test takers are not expected to present any new ideas in their essays. Instead, test takers must summarize the lecture and explain its relationship with the reading passage by providing examples from both.

ABOUT THE
TOEFL® iBT
WRITING SECTION

There are five possible writing tasks test takers will be presented with, but they all require test takers to summarize the lecture and to explain how it either supports or contradicts the reading.

If the listening passage challenges or contradicts the reading passage, the tasks will be presented in one of the following ways:

- Summarize the points made in the lecture, being sure to explain how they cast doubt on specific points made in the reading passage.
  cf. This question type accounts for most of the questions that have been asked on the TOEFL® iBT so far.
- Summarize the points made in the lecture, being sure to explain how they challenge specific claims/arguments made in the reading passage.
- Summarize the points made in the lecture, being sure to specifically explain how they answer the problems raised in the reading passage.

If the listening passage supports or strengthens the reading passage, the tasks will be presented in one of the following ways:

- Summarize the points made in the lecture, being sure to specifically explain how they support the explanations in the reading passage.
- Summarize the points made in the lecture, being sure to specifically explain how they strengthen specific points made in the reading passage.

TYPE 2 The Independent Writing Task

The Independent Writing Task is the second half of the TOEFL® iBT writing section. Test takers have 30 minutes to write an essay explaining their options about a given question. Typically, an effective response is between 300 and 400 words in length. In order to earn a top score, test takers must clearly present their ideas by using logical arguments and effective supporting examples. Strong responses generally include an introductory paragraph with a clear thesis statement, two or three supporting paragraphs with focused topic sentences, and a brief concluding paragraph.

There are three possible writing tasks you will be presented with, but they all ask you to express your opinion about an important issue.

For the agree/disagree type, the task will be presented in the following way:

- Do you agree or disagree with the following statement?
  [A sentence or sentences that present an issue]
  Use specific reasons and examples to support your answer.
  cf. This question type accounts for most of the essay topics that have been asked on the TOEFL® iBT so far.

For the preference type, the task will be presented in the following way:

- Some people prefer X. Others prefer Y. Which do you prefer? Use specific reasons and examples to support your choice.

For the opinion type, the task will be presented in the following way:

- [A sentence or sentences that state a fact]
  In your opinion, what is one thing that should be . . . ? Use specific reasons and examples to support your answer.

HOW TO USE THIS BOOK

Decoding the TOEFL® iBT Writing Intermediate is designed to be used either as a textbook in a classroom environment or as a study guide for individual learners. There are 2 parts with 10 chapters each in this book. Each chapter provides 2 sample tasks or questions. There are 4 or 5 sections in each chapter, which enable you to build up your skills on a particular writing task. At the end of the book, there is one actual test of the Writing section of the TOEFL® iBT.

Part A Integrated Writing Task

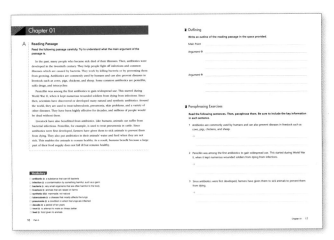

A ｜ Reading Passage

This section contains a reading passage between 200 and 250 words long. There is a vocabulary section with definitions of difficult words or phrases in the passage. There are also sections for outlining and paraphrasing to make sure you understand the material you read and can condense it.

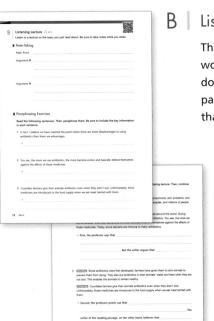

B ｜ Listening Lecture

This section contains a listening lecture between 200 and 250 words long. There is a section for note-taking so that you can write down the key information you hear in the lecture. There is also a paraphrasing section to make sure you can condense the information that you heard.

C ｜ Combining the Main Points

This section contains 2 or 3 excerpts each from the reading passage and listening lecture. You should read the excerpts and then use the information in them to complete each sentence. Then, complete the sample essay on the next page by using the outline you wrote and the notes you took.

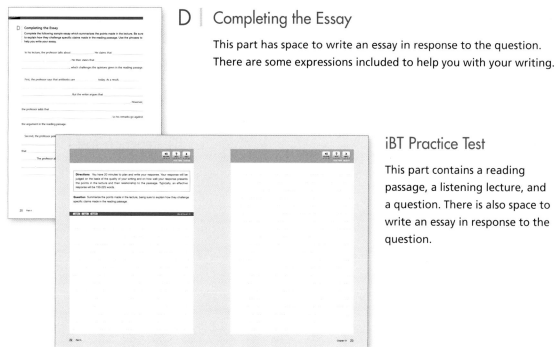

D | Completing the Essay

This part has space to write an essay in response to the question. There are some expressions included to help you with your writing.

iBT Practice Test

This part contains a reading passage, a listening lecture, and a question. There is also space to write an essay in response to the question.

Part B | Independent Writing Task

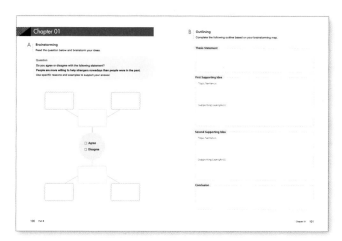

A | Brainstorming

This section contains a question and space for brainstorming to prepare to write your answer.

B | Outlining

This part has space for an outline that will describe what information will be included in the introduction, body, and conclusion of the essay.

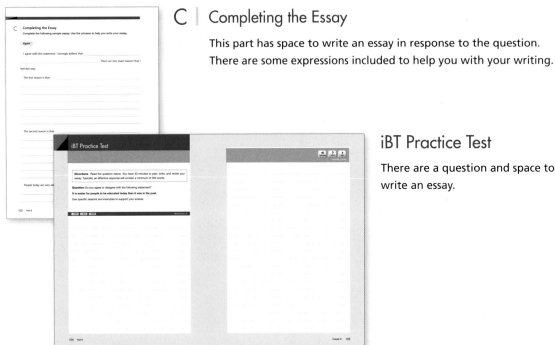

C | Completing the Essay

This part has space to write an essay in response to the question. There are some expressions included to help you with your writing.

iBT Practice Test

There are a question and space to write an essay.

● **Actual Test** (at the end of the book)

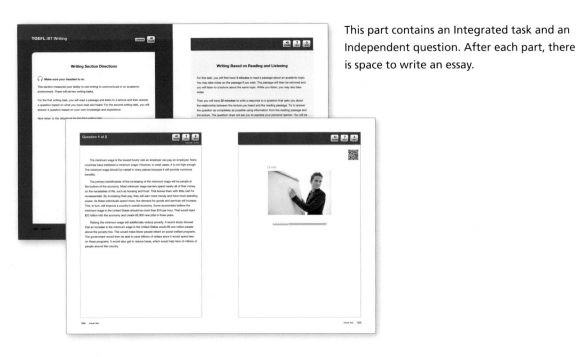

This part contains an Integrated task and an Independent question. After each part, there is space to write an essay.

Part **A**

Integrated Writing Task

Integrated Writing Task

◪ About the Question

The Integrated Writing Task contains three parts. The first part is a reading passage that is around 230 to 300 words long. You are given 3 minutes to read the passage. Next, you will hear a lecture that either supports the reading passage or goes against it in some manner. Last, you will be given 20 minutes to write an essay on the reading passage and listening lecture. Your essay should be 150 to 225 words long. While you are writing your essay, you will be able to see the reading passage on the screen. To write your essay, simply provide a summary of the lecture and explain how it is connected to the reading passage. You should be sure to use the examples that are provided in the two passages. However, avoid using any new ideas or examples that do not appear in either of the passages. Your essay must be taken solely from the information presented in the two passages.

There are five possible writing tasks that may be presented to you. All of them require that you summarize the lecture and explain how it supports or goes against the reading passage. The vast majority of passages have the lecture contradicting, casting doubt on, or challenging the issues that are mentioned in the reading passage. Very few lectures support the reading passage.

If the listening passage challenges or contradicts the reading passage, the tasks will be presented in one of the following ways:

- Summarize the points made in the lecture, being sure to explain how they cast doubt on specific points made in the reading.

  cf. This question type accounts for most of the questions that have been asked on the TOEFL® iBT so far.

- Summarize the points made in the lecture, being sure to explain how they challenge specific claims/arguments made in the reading.

- Summarize the points made in the lecture, being sure to specifically explain how they answer the problems raised in the reading passage.

If the listening passage supports or strengthens the reading passage, the tasks will be presented in one of the following ways:

- Summarize the points made in the lecture, being sure to specifically explain how they support the explanations in the reading passage.

- Summarize the points made in the lecture, being sure to specifically explain how they strengthen specific points made in the reading passage.

■ Sample Question

The American pika is a small mammal which resembles a rodent but is actually related to the rabbit. It lives in mountainous regions in the western part of the United States. It is typically seen above the treeline in rocky areas with cliffs. In recent years, its numbers have been declining. Most of the blame for this has to do with rising temperature levels.

The pika's body has evolved so that it retains heat well. It has thick fur and a round shape. Both of these are ideal characteristics for keeping heat in the body. In the past, the mountainous regions where it mostly lives were cold nearly all year round. The temperatures rarely rose above the freezing level. But the temperatures in these areas have increased lately, so the pika's body is overheating. When the temperature is only twenty-five degrees Celsius, it can die because the temperature is too warm.

An additional problem is that the changing weather is affecting the pika's environment. The pika eats vegetation which grows at high altitudes. The animal collects vegetation in summer and stores the food in its den for the winter. But the temperature changes are causing new types of vegetation to grow at higher altitudes. This new vegetation is replacing the pika's natural food sources. So the animal has less access to the food it is accustomed to eating. Many pikas are therefore starving due to a lack of food.

🎧 A00

| Script | **M Professor:** Look at your books, please. That is a picture of an American pika. This small, fur-covered cousin of the rabbit is an endangered species. In eight of the twenty-five mountainous regions it once highly populated, it has disappeared. It's declining in the other areas. Some biologists claim that rising temperatures are killing the pika, but, well, I'm skeptical of their claims.

Now, um, it's true that the pika can die if its core body temperature increases too much. But please note that the snow in the mountains where the pika lives melts every year. The pika has lived in these conditions for a long time without dying out. It can also hide in the shade or retreat to deep dens on hot days. So, uh, it has ways to counter the summer heat to keep from dying.

Some biologists claim that the pika's ecosystem is changing because new vegetation is growing in this area. Well, they're right about the change in the environment; however, the new vegetation shouldn't be killing the pika. The reason is simple: It's not a specialized eater. It eats everything, including, uh, wild grasses, weeds, hay, and flowers. So there shouldn't be any problem with its food supply. In fact, since the weather is getting warmer and more plants are growing, the pika is actually seeing an increase in its food supply rather than a decrease.

Directions You have 20 minutes to plan and write your response. Your response will be judged on the basis of the quality of your writing and on how well your response presents the points in the lecture and their relationship to the passage. Typically, an effective response will be 150-225 words.

Question Summarize the points made in the lecture, being sure to explain how they cast doubt on specific points made in the reading passage.

Sample Essay

The professor lectures on the pika, an animal which lives in the United States. The author of the reading passage believes that temperature changes are the problem. Yet the professor claims that the rising temperature is not the reason its numbers are declining.

The professor first points out that the pika does not react well to heat. In this way, he agrees with the reading passage. It states that the pika retains heat well and can die when the temperature gets to twenty-five degrees Celsius. However, the professor mentions that the temperature always rises in summer, but the pika has survived for many years. He also contends that the animal can rest in the shade or in dens to avoid the heat.

Next, the professor discusses the pika's food supply. The author of the reading passage believes this is a problem. Because the weather is getting hotter, new types of vegetation are growing in the pika's environment. Therefore, the pika cannot consume its normal food, so it is starving. The professor disregards this argument, too. He states that the pika is not a picky eater but will instead eat anything. So he thinks that the animal's food supply is increasing in size rather than decreasing.

Chapter 01

A   Reading Passage

Read the following passage carefully. Try to understand what the main argument of the passage is.

In the past, many people who became sick died of their illnesses. Then, antibiotics were developed in the twentieth century. They help people fight off infections and common illnesses which are caused by bacteria. They work by killing bacteria or by preventing them from growing. Antibiotics are commonly used by humans and can also prevent diseases in livestock such as cows, pigs, chickens, and sheep. Some common antibiotics are penicillin, sulfa drugs, and tetracycline.

Penicillin was among the first antibiotics to gain widespread use. This started during World War II, when it kept numerous wounded soldiers from dying from infections. Since then, scientists have discovered or developed many natural and synthetic antibiotics. Around the world, they are used to treat tuberculosis, pneumonia, skin problems, and a variety of other diseases. They have been highly effective for decades, and millions of people would be dead without them.

Livestock have also benefitted from antibiotics. Like humans, animals can suffer from bacterial infections. Penicillin, for example, is used to treat pneumonia in cattle. Since antibiotics were first developed, farmers have given them to sick animals to prevent them from dying. They also put antibiotics in their animals' water and feed when they are not sick. This enables the animals to remain healthy. As a result, humans benefit because a large part of their food supply does not fall ill but remains healthy.

Vocabulary

- **antibiotic** *n* a substance that can kill bacteria
- **infection** *n* a contamination by something harmful, such as a germ
- **bacteria** *n* very small organisms that are often harmful to the body
- **livestock** *n* animals that are raised on farms
- **synthetic** *adj* manmade; not natural
- **tuberculosis** *n* a disease that mostly affects the lungs
- **pneumonia** *n* a condition in which the lungs are inflamed
- **decade** *n* a period of ten years
- **treat** *v* to attempt to make an illness better
- **feed** *n* food given to animals

◪ Outlining

Write an outline of the reading passage in the space provided.

Main Point _____

Argument ❶ _____

_____

_____

Argument ❷ _____

_____

_____

◪ Paraphrasing Exercises

Read the following sentences. Then, paraphrase them. Be sure to include the key information in each sentence.

1 Antibiotics are commonly used by humans and can also prevent diseases in livestock such as cows, pigs, chickens, and sheep.

→ _____

_____

2 Penicillin was among the first antibiotics to gain widespread use. This started during World War II, when it kept numerous wounded soldiers from dying from infections.

→ _____

_____

3 Since antibiotics were first developed, farmers have given them to sick animals to prevent them from dying.

→ _____

_____

B | Listening Lecture 🎧 A01

Listen to a lecture on the topic you just read about. Be sure to take notes while you listen.

◪ Note-Taking

Main Point   _____

Argument ❶   _____

_____

_____

Argument ❷   _____

_____

_____

◪ Paraphrasing Exercises

Read the following sentences. Then, paraphrase them. Be sure to include the key information in each sentence.

1   In fact, I believe we have reached the point where there are more disadvantages to using antibiotics than there are advantages.

→ _____

_____

2   You see, the more we use antibiotics, the more bacteria evolve and basically defend themselves against the effects of these medicines.

→ _____

_____

3   Countless farmers give their animals antibiotics even when they aren't sick. Unfortunately, those medicines are introduced to the food supply when we eat meat tainted with them.

→ _____

_____

C | Combining the Main Points

Read the following sentences from the reading passage and listening lecture. Then, combine each pair of sentences by using the given patterns.

1 **Reading** Around the world, they are used to treat tuberculosis, pneumonia, skin problems, and a variety of other diseases. They have been highly effective for decades, and millions of people would be dead without them.

Listening Since the 1940s, antibiotics have been commonly used around the world. During that time, bacteria have begun developing resistance to some antibiotics. You see, the more we use antibiotics, the more bacteria evolve and basically defend themselves against the effects of these medicines. Today, some bacteria are immune to many antibiotics.

→ **First, the professor says that** _____

_____

_____ **. But the writer argues that** _____

_____ .

2 **Reading** Since antibiotics were first developed, farmers have given them to sick animals to prevent them from dying. They also put antibiotics in their animals' water and feed when they are not sick. This enables the animals to remain healthy.

Listening Countless farmers give their animals antibiotics even when they aren't sick. Unfortunately, those medicines are introduced to the food supply when we eat meat tainted with them.

→ **Second, the professor points out that** _____

_____ **. The**

writer of the reading passage, on the other hand, believes that _____

_____ .

D Completing the Essay

Complete the following sample essay which summarizes the points made in the lecture. Be sure to explain how they challenge specific claims made in the reading passage. Use the phrases to help you write your essay.

In his lecture, the professor talks about _____ . He claims that _____

_____ . He then states that _____

_____ , which challenges the opinions given in the reading passage.

First, the professor says that antibiotics are _____ today. As a result, _____

_____

_____ . But the writer argues that _____

_____ . However,

the professor adds that _____

_____ . So his remarks go against

the argument in the reading passage.

Second, the professor points out that _____ . This causes

_____ . The writer of the reading passage, on the other hand, believes

that _____

_____ . The professor also remarks that _____

_____ . _____

_____ .

The roads of the future will not be made of asphalt. Instead, they will be solar roads. They will have surfaces comprised of solar panels which will absorb sunlight. These panels will then generate power for the lighting alongside the roads and make energy for charging stations for electric vehicles. While many people are skeptical about the possibility of making solar roads, scientists are positive they can build them.

First, the solar panels to be used for solar roads will be made of tempered glass. They will be strong enough to resist damage from vehicles moving over them, so they will not shatter due to excessive weight. They will also not be affected by rain or snow. In fact, solar road systems will be able to heat roads. They will melt any ice and snow on them, thereby making driving conditions safer. Finally, solar roads will not suffer damage because of inclement weather. As a result, they will have no cracks and potholes.

Second, while building the roads will be expensive, they will save money after a few years. There will be no need to repair potholes. Thus maintenance costs will be much lower. In addition, when electric vehicles recharge by using the electricity created by solar roads, the users can be charged fees. That will enable solar roads to make money, which should please taxpayers in the regions they are used.

🎧 A02

Directions You have 20 minutes to plan and write your response. Your response will be judged on the basis of the quality of your writing and on how well your response presents the points in the lecture and their relationship to the passage. Typically, an effective response will be 150-225 words.

Question Summarize the points made in the lecture, being sure to explain how they challenge specific claims made in the reading passage.

COPY   CUT   PASTE   Word Count : 0

A Reading Passage

Read the following passage carefully. Try to understand what the main argument of the passage is.

Scattered around Scotland are the remains of tall, round stone towers called brochs. They were built between the years 800 B.C. and 200 A.D. This was during the Iron Age in Scotland. Each tower had a double outer wall of stone and a hollow interior. Some had wooden floors and stone staircases leading up to higher levels. They had no windows and a single door.

The main purpose of brochs remains a matter of debate. One theory accepted by many scholars is that brochs served as fortifications. Many are located at strategic points where invaders were likely to attack. It is likely that when enemy soldiers arrived, locals fled to the brochs and held off the attackers from them. Built with stone, brochs were sturdy. If the people inside had enough food, they could easily withstand a siege.

A second theory many people believe is that local leaders lived in brochs. Essentially, they were simple castles, and the lords living in them ruled the people nearby. The brochs were therefore symbols of power and prestige. When brochs were built, most people lived in primitive housing, so the tall brochs must have looked impressive. There are also the remains of other buildings at some broch sites. It is possible that they served as central points for the growth of villages in Scotland 2,000 years ago.

Vocabulary

- **remains** *n* ruins; the destroyed parts of an old building
- **hollow** *adj* having nothing in one's center
- **staircase** *n* a stairway
- **serve** *v* to act as
- **strategic** *adj* tactical; important
- **flee** *v* to run away; to escape from
- **essentially** *adv* basically; for the most part
- **prestige** *n* a good reputation
- **primitive** *adj* basic; simple
- **village** *n* a very small town

◪ Outlining

Write an outline of the reading passage in the space provided.

Main Point _____

Argument ❶ _____

_____

_____

Argument ❷ _____

_____

_____

◪ Paraphrasing Exercises

Read the following sentences. Then, paraphrase them. Be sure to include the key information in each sentence.

1 Scattered around Scotland are the remains of tall, round stone towers called brochs. They were built between the years 800 B.C. and 200 A.D.

→ _____

_____

2 It is likely that when enemy soldiers arrived, locals fled to the brochs and held off the attackers from them.

→ _____

_____

3 When brochs were built, most people lived in primitive housing, so the tall brochs must have looked impressive.

→ _____

_____

B │ Listening Lecture 🎧 A03

Listen to a lecture on the topic you just read about. Be sure to take notes while you listen.

◢ Note-Taking

Main Point _____

Argument ❶ _____

_____

_____

_____

Argument ❷ _____

_____

_____

_____

◢ Paraphrasing Exercises

Read the following sentences. Then, paraphrase them. Be sure to include the key information in each sentence.

1 The remains of approximately 500 of these stone towers have been found in various parts of Scotland.

   → _____

   _____

2 No windows meant that the people inside couldn't see any attackers outside. Nor could they fire at attackers from inside with spears or arrows since there were no windows to shoot from.

   → _____

   _____

3 The only problem with that theory is that out of around 500 broch sites, evidence of large nearby populations has been found in fewer than two dozen places.

   → _____

C | Combining the Main Points

Read the following sentences from the reading passage and listening lecture. Then, combine each pair of sentences by using the given patterns.

1 `Reading` It is likely that when enemy soldiers arrived, locals fled to the brochs and held off the attackers from them. Built with stone, brochs were sturdy. If the people inside had enough food, they could easily withstand a siege.

`Listening` Notice the lack of windows and the single entrance. No windows meant that the people inside couldn't see any attackers outside. Nor could they fire at attackers from inside with spears or arrows since there were no windows to shoot from.

→ **According to the reading passage,** _____

_____ **. The professor disregards**

this notion. She says that _____

_____ .

2 `Reading` A second theory many people believe is that local leaders lived in brochs. Essentially, they were simple castles, and the lords living in them ruled the people nearby.

`Listening` This has caused many people to speculate that local strongmen and their families dwelled in brochs. The only problem with that theory is that out of around 500 broch sites, evidence of large nearby populations has been found in fewer than two dozen places.

→ **The reading passage argues that** _____

_____ **, but the professor does not think so. She claims that** _____

_____ .

D | Completing the Essay

Complete the following sample essay which summarizes the points made in the lecture. Be sure to explain how they cast doubt on specific points made in the reading passage. Use the phrases to help you write your essay.

The professor lectures on brochs in Scotland. They were _____

_____ . During her lecture, she mentions _____

_____ .

The first theory she discusses is that _____ . According to the

reading passage, _____

_____ . The professor disregards this notion. She says that _____

_____ . She adds

that _____ .

And she states that _____ .

The second theory she casts doubt on is that _____

_____ . The reading passage argues that _____

_____ , but the professor does not think so. She claims that _____

_____ . Furthermore, she mentions that_____

_____ . Therefore, she does not believe that

_____ .

In the southeastern part of Greece near Argos is a structure called the Pyramid of Hellinikon. It is rather small, being around seven by ten meters in area. It stands three and a half meters high. A corridor leads to a single square room that is open to the sky since the roof no longer exists. The entire structure is made from large blocks of gray limestone. Archaeologists have dated it to about 2700 B.C.

Most pyramids in ancient times served as tombs, and many people believe the Pyramid of Hellinikon was one, too. According to some Greek texts, a great battle once took place near the site. It ended in a draw, and the two sides stopped fighting the war after the battle. They buried their dead in the area, and then they built the pyramid together. The pyramid, which once had carvings of shields on the outside, served as both a tomb and memorial of the battle.

A second theory is that the pyramid was a fort for a small group of soldiers. It is hypothesized that the missing roof was flat. That allowed soldiers to stand on it to observe the countryside. Archaeologists have unearthed pottery shards at the site. They date from many time periods in both Greek history and Roman times. This indicates that the area was continually occupied by people, most likely soldiers.

🎧 A04

Directions You have 20 minutes to plan and write your response. Your response will be judged on the basis of the quality of your writing and on how well your response presents the points in the lecture and their relationship to the passage. Typically, an effective response will be 150-225 words.

Question Summarize the points made in the lecture, being sure to explain how they challenge specific arguments made in the reading passage.

COPY   CUT   PASTE   Word Count : 0

Chapter 03

A Reading Passage

Read the following passage carefully. Try to understand what the main argument of the passage is.

An extinction-level event is one that kills the majority of life on the Earth. There have been several in the planet's history. The best-known one took place sixty-five million years ago. Then, an asteroid hit the planet and killed most of the dinosaurs. It is possible that more asteroids will hit the planet in the future. That is why space organizations such as NASA search the skies for potentially deadly objects.

NASA's Near-Earth Object (NEO) team uses various methods to find and track large asteroids. The main instruments are ground-based telescopes and satellites in space. The satellites are capable of observing very dark objects that reflect little light. So far, NASA's team has observed more than 75% of the space near the Earth and has detected more than 25,000 objects. These include large asteroids and comets.

NASA then uses the information to warn the public about NEOs that are coming close to the planet. If a large one is on target to hit the Earth, there are several ways to deal with it. A nuclear missile could strike it and send it off course. Heavy rockets could collide with it to change its course as well. Or space-based lasers could destroy parts of the NEO and change its path. These methods would all be able to prevent an extinction-level event from happening on the Earth again.

Vocabulary

- □ **majority** _n_ most; a number more than half of a total
- □ **asteroid** _n_ a large, rocky object that orbits the sun
- □ **potentially** _adv_ possibly
- □ **telescope** _n_ a tool that can look closely at distant objects
- □ **observe** _v_ to see; to look at
- □ **reflect** _v_ to throw back from a surface
- □ **detect** _v_ to find
- □ **comet** _n_ a large ball of ice and dirt that orbits the sun
- □ **collide** _v_ to hit; to run into
- □ **prevent** _v_ to stop from happening

◪ Outlining

Write an outline of the reading passage in the space provided.

Main Point   _____

Argument ❶   _____

                         _____

                         _____

Argument ❷   _____

                         _____

                         _____

◪ Paraphrasing Exercises

Read the following sentences. Then, paraphrase them. Be sure to include the key information in each sentence.

1 It is possible that more asteroids will hit the planet in the future. That is why space organizations such as NASA search the skies for potentially deadly objects.

  → _____

     _____

2 NASA's Near-Earth Object (NEO) team uses various methods to find and track large asteroids. The main instruments are ground-based telescopes and satellites in space.

  → _____

     _____

3 A nuclear missile could strike it and send it off course. Heavy rockets could collide with it to change its course as well. Or space-based lasers could destroy parts of the NEO and change its path.

  → _____

     _____

B | Listening Lecture A05

Listen to a lecture on the topic you just read about. Be sure to take notes while you listen.

Note-Taking

Main Point ______________________

Argument ❶ ______________________

____

____

Argument ❷ ______________________

____

____

Paraphrasing Exercises

Read the following sentences. Then, paraphrase them. Be sure to include the key information in each sentence.

1 If an asteroid struck the planet, it could cause massive amounts of damage. If it's large enough, it could cause humans and other species to go extinct.

→ ______________________

____

2 Sadly, ground-based telescopes aren't very efficient. They have trouble finding objects since the asteroids are fairly small and therefore don't reflect much light. Satellites are better, but they're expensive and can't identify every asteroid.

→ ______________________

____

3 The only one that might work at this point is nuclear missiles. But if the asteroid is several miles in diameter, missiles will be useless.

→ ______________________

____

C | Combining the Main Points

Read the following sentences from the reading passage and listening lecture. Then, combine each pair of sentences by using the given patterns.

1   **Reading** The main instruments are ground-based telescopes and satellites in space. The satellites are capable of observing very dark objects that reflect little light. So far, NASA's team has observed more than 75% of the space near the Earth and has detected more than 25,000 objects.

   Listening Sadly, ground-based telescopes aren't very efficient. They have trouble finding objects since the asteroids are fairly small and therefore don't reflect much light. Satellites are better, but they're expensive and can't identify every asteroid.

   → **The author of the reading passage notes that** _____

   _____ **. According to the passage,** _____

   _____ **. The professor disagrees with**

   this assertion. He says that _____

   _____ .

2   **Reading** A nuclear missile could strike it and send it off course. Heavy rockets could collide with it to change its course as well. Or space-based lasers could destroy parts of the NEO and change its path.

   Listening Sure, there are plans to use missiles, rockets, and lasers. But none has been tested. They're only plans on drawing boards right now. The only one that might work at this point is nuclear missiles.

   → **The author of the reading passage mentions that** _____

   _____ **, but the professor disagrees. He declares that** _____

   _____ .

D | Completing the Essay

Complete the following sample essay which summarizes the points made in the lecture. Be sure to explain how they cast doubt on specific points made in the reading passage. Use the phrases to help you write your essay.

Both the lecture and the reading passage are about _____

_____. While the author of the reading passage believes _____,

the professor _____.

First, the professor talks about _____. The author of the reading passage notes that

_____. According to the

passage, _____. The professor

disagrees with this assertion. He says that _____

_____. He also

points out that _____

_____. He thinks _____.

Second, the professor claims that _____

_____. The author of the reading passage mentions that _____

_____, but the professor disagrees. He declares

that _____. But he

adds that _____.

Colonizing Mars will not be simple, but several organizations are making plans to attempt to do so. To accomplish their mission, they first need to send a team on a months-long journey to Mars. Afterward, those astronauts must establish a colony to ensure that they and others can survive on the planet.

The journey itself will be difficult, but the obstacles can be overcome. On a long journey, the crew will be exposed to radiation in space. However, if the crew departs when Earth and Mars are close to each other, the trip will only take seven months. During that time, the astronauts will not be exposed to enough radiation to cause harm. Some people are concerned about the physical and mental health of the crew due to the lengthy journey. However, astronauts have spent long amounts of time on space stations and only suffered minor problems, so a trip to Mars should be no different.

On Mars, the astronauts can live in prefabricated housing units for years. Those units will protect them from radiation. As for food, they can bring preserved food, and rockets resupplying them can arrive from Earth. The astronauts can also grow plants on Mars to provide both food and oxygen. As for water, it can be recycled, and there are also places with frozen water on Mars. Thus, all the necessities of life are attainable on Mars.

A06

Directions You have 20 minutes to plan and write your response. Your response will be judged on the basis of the quality of your writing and on how well your response presents the points in the lecture and their relationship to the passage. Typically, an effective response will be 150-225 words.

Question Summarize the points made in the lecture, being sure to explain how they challenge specific claims made in the reading passage.

COPY   CUT   PASTE   Word Count : 0

A | Reading Passage

Read the following passage carefully. Try to understand what the main argument of the passage is.

In recent years, there has been a trend for cities to build airports far from their downtown areas. Government officials constantly make statements that these locations in suburban or rural sites are ideal. However, that is far from the truth. Instead, having airports located inside large cities is much better.

Airports located within city limits are convenient for passengers to get to. When passengers live closer to airports, they can arrive at their destinations much faster and more easily. This saves them both time and money. Many travelers also make use of existing public transportation networks to get to airports. Having airports downtown enables cities to avoid building expensive subway or train lines to airports outside the city limits. Nor do cities need to construct new roads leading to distant airports. All of these measures save money, which benefits taxpayers.

In the past, people often complained about noise levels from airports located inside cities. Airplanes taking off and landing at all hours of the day and night annoyed numerous residents. However, this issue has been solved nowadays. Airplanes now take flight paths over the least populated areas of cities. In addition, most airports in cities are not located near residential areas. Instead, they are typically found near factories and other businesses. As a result, the noise airplanes create disturbs as few people as possible.

Vocabulary

- □ **trend** (n) a style; something that has become popular with many people
- □ **suburban** (adj) relating to the suburbs or a place near a large city
- □ **rural** (adj) relating to the countryside
- □ **destination** (n) the place one is going
- □ **network** (n) a system containing individual parts that work together as a single unit
- □ **enable** (v) to let happen; to permit
- □ **taxpayer** (n) a person who pays taxes to the government
- □ **annoy** (v) to bother
- □ **populated** (adj) having people living in a certain area
- □ **disturb** (v) to bother

◪ Outlining

Write an outline of the reading passage in the space provided.

Main Point

Argument ❶

Argument ❷

◪ Paraphrasing Exercises

Read the following sentences. Then, paraphrase them. Be sure to include the key information in each sentence.

1 Government officials constantly make statements that these locations in suburban or rural sites are ideal. However, that is far from the truth.

→

2 Having airports downtown enables cities to avoid building expensive subway or train lines to airports outside the city limits.

→

3 In the past, people often complained about noise levels from airports located inside cities. Airplanes taking off and landing at all hours of the day and night annoyed numerous residents.

→

B | Listening Lecture 🎧 A07

Listen to a lecture on the topic you just read about. Be sure to take notes while you listen.

▌ Note-Taking

Main Point _____

Argument ❶ _____

_____

_____

Argument ❷ _____

_____

_____

▌ Paraphrasing Exercises

Read the following sentences. Then, paraphrase them. Be sure to include the key information in each sentence.

1 Personally, I think the city should close the airport downtown and build an entirely new one outside the city limits.

→ _____

_____

2 But if the city purchases unused land in the countryside, it will be much cheaper. It can obtain a huge amount of land that it can use both now and later in the future for a second expansion.

→ _____

_____

3 If we build an airport in an out-of-the-way place, we won't have to worry about noise pollution in the city limits anymore.

→ _____

_____

C | Combining the Main Points

Read the following sentences from the reading passage and listening lecture. Then, combine each pair of sentences by using the given patterns.

1 **Reading** When passengers live closer to airports, they can arrive at their destinations much faster and more easily. This saves them both time and money. Many travelers also make use of existing public transportation networks to get to airports. Having airports downtown enables cities to avoid building expensive subway or train lines to airports outside the city limits.

Listening But if the city purchases unused land in the countryside, it will be much cheaper. It can obtain a huge amount of land that it can use both now and later in the future for a second expansion.

→ **The professor's arguments are against those in the reading passage. It states that** _____

_____ . **It also notes**

that _____

The professor counters by mentioning that _____

_____ .

2 **Reading** Airplanes now take flight paths over the least populated areas of cities. In addition, most airports in cities are not located near residential areas. Instead, they are typically found near factories and other businesses.

Listening Airplanes fly over my house all the time. Sometimes they're so loud that I can't have a conversation in my own house. If we build an airport in an out-of-the-way place, we won't have to worry about noise pollution in the city limits anymore.

→ **Again, the professor's opinion opposes the argument made in the reading passage. It**

claims that _____

_____ . **The professor, however, complains**

about _____ .

D Completing the Essay

Complete the following sample essay which summarizes the points made in the lecture. Be sure to explain how they challenge specific arguments made in the reading passage. Use the phrases to help you write your essay.

The lecture and the reading passage are both about _____ . While the reading

passage _____ , the professor _____ .

The first argument the professor makes against downtown airports is _____ . Her

arguments are against those in the reading passage. It states that _____

_____ . It also notes that _____

_____ . The professor counters by mentioning that _____

_____ . She stresses

that _____

_____ .

The second argument she makes concerns _____ . Again, the professor's opinion opposes the

argument made in the reading passage. It claims that _____

_____ .

_____ . The professor, however, complains about _____

_____ .

_____

_____ .

Inflation is the rate at which the prices of goods and services rise. Many factors, including the demand for goods and services, can cause inflation. For instance, when people have money to spend and the supply of goods is low, sellers can charge high prices for them.

While inflation may seem bad, it has some positive characteristics. Economists consider an annual inflation rate of two percent a sign of a healthy economy. When an economy is growing, there is normally demand for products. This can cause prices to rise somewhat. However, since people are employed and making money, this minor inflation rate is acceptable. For instance, from the late 1990s to early 2000s, the economy of the United States often grew between four and six percent each year. The inflation rate was usually around two or three percent. This showed the healthiness of the American economy.

A second benefit of inflation concerns individuals who borrow money from banks. When the inflation rate is higher than the interest rates people are paying on loans, they benefit. The reason concerns the real value of money. For example, perhaps a person borrows $1,000, but the inflation rate rises. When the borrower pays the money back later, that $1,000 is worth less than it was previously. Thus borrowers can be encouraged by high rates of inflation to borrow large sums of money.

🎧 A08

Directions You have 20 minutes to plan and write your response. Your response will be judged on the basis of the quality of your writing and on how well your response presents the points in the lecture and their relationship to the passage. Typically, an effective response will be 150-225 words.

Question Summarize the points made in the lecture, being sure to explain how they challenge specific arguments made in the reading passage.

COPY   CUT   PASTE   Word Count : 0

A   Reading Passage

Read the following passage carefully. Try to understand what the main argument of the passage is.

The sea turtle is close to extinction as six of its seven species are endangered. This animal, which lives in warm and temperate waters, spends the majority of its life at sea. There are two primary reasons for the decline in its population. So people are focusing on those issues in an effort to preserve them.

Sea turtles often get caught in fishermen's nets and drown. To prevent this, some countries have passed laws banning fishing in areas where sea turtles live in great numbers. In addition, some fishing nets have turtle excluder devices. They are made of metal bars and prevent large animals, such as sea turtles, from entering the main net through the net's entrance tunnel. The devices allow small creatures to go into the nets. But they let sea turtles escape, which prevents turtles from needlessly dying.

The other major problem is that people enjoy eating sea turtles and their eggs. As a result, the turtles are hunted, and their eggs are collected. In Costa Rica and Mexico, beaches where turtles lay their eggs are protected areas, so people are not allowed on them. Both countries have also passed laws making it illegal to catch sea turtles and to harvest their eggs. And there are efforts to educate local populations to make people aware that sea turtles are in danger of going extinct.

Vocabulary

- □ **extinction** n no longer in existence as a species
- □ **endangered** adj being in danger of going extinct; having very low numbers
- □ **temperate** adj mild
- □ **primary** adj main
- □ **drown** v to die due to taking in too much water
- □ **ban** v not to permit an activity; to make an activity against the law
- □ **device** n a piece of equipment
- □ **hunt** v to find and to try to kill
- □ **illegal** adj against the law
- □ **harvest** v to collect food

◾ Outlining

Write an outline of the reading passage in the space provided.

Main Point _____

Argument ❶ _____

_____

_____

Argument ❷ _____

_____

_____

◾ Paraphrasing Exercises

Read the following sentences. Then, paraphrase them. Be sure to include the key information in each sentence.

1 There are two primary reasons for the decline in its population. So people are focusing on those issues in an effort to preserve them.

→ _____

_____

2 In addition, some fishing nets have turtle excluder devices. They are made of metal bars and prevent large animals, such as sea turtles, from entering the main net through the net's entrance tunnel.

→ _____

_____

3 In Costa Rica and Mexico, beaches where turtles lay their eggs are protected areas, so people are not allowed on them.

→ _____

_____

B | Listening Lecture 🎧 A09

Listen to a lecture on the topic you just read about. Be sure to take notes while you listen.

◼ Note-Taking

Main Point _____

Argument ❶ _____

_____

_____

Argument ❷ _____

_____

_____

◼ Paraphrasing Exercises

Read the following sentences. Then, paraphrase them. Be sure to include the key information in each sentence.

1 While there are ongoing efforts to help the turtle, they are not, well . . . they're not entirely effective.

→ _____

_____

2 I'm aware of the special nets that can allow turtles to escape. But fishermen dislike them since they let fish and other creatures get out as well.

→ _____

_____

3 People will pay big money for them, so there are always individuals willing to break the law to catch the turtles and to collect their eggs.

→ _____

_____

C | Combining the Main Points

Read the following sentences from the reading passage and listening lecture. Then, combine each pair of sentences by using the given patterns.

1 **Reading** Sea turtles often get caught in fishermen's nets and drown. To prevent this, some countries have passed laws banning fishing in areas where sea turtles live in great numbers.

Listening Not enough countries have banned fishing in areas where sea turtles live. Even in places where it is banned, fishermen break the law and fish in those spots.

→ **The professor talks about** _____ **. She points**

out that _____ **. She adds**

that _____ **. This is in contrast**

to the reading passage. It claims that _____

_____ **.**

2 **Reading** In Costa Rica and Mexico, beaches where turtles lay their eggs are protected areas, so people are not allowed on them. Both countries have also passed laws making it illegal to catch sea turtles and to harvest their eggs.

Listening Another issue is that sea turtle meat and eggs are considered delicacies around the world. People will pay big money for them, so there are always individuals willing to break the law to catch the turtles and to collect their eggs.

→ **Next, the professor covers** _____ **.**

_____

_____ **. On the other hand, the reading passage notes that** _____

_____ **.**

D | Completing the Essay

Complete the following sample essay which summarizes the points made in the lecture. Be sure to explain how they cast doubt on specific points made in the reading passage. Use the phrases to help you write your essay.

Both the lecture and the reading passage are about _____

_____ . While the reading passage is positive about _____

_____ , the professor is more negative.

The professor talks about _____ . She points out that

_____ . She adds that _____

_____ . This is in contrast to the reading

passage. It claims that _____ .

The reading passage also states that _____

_____ . But the professor mentions that _____

_____ .

Next, the professor covers _____ . _____

_____ .

On the other hand, the reading passage notes that _____

_____ . But the professor argues that _____

_____ .

The Gulf sturgeon is a large fish that dwells in the northern part of the Gulf of Mexico and coastal rivers. It winters in the gulf and swims into rivers to spawn in spring. The sturgeon is noted for its ability to jump high out of the water while in rivers. There are two theories concerning this habit.

Some speculate that the fish leaps to suck in air in order to refill its swim bladder. This air-filled bladder allows the sturgeon to have neutral buoyancy in the water. It can thereby remain in one place underwater. As the fish spends time resting at the bottoms of rivers in summer and fall, air slowly leaks from its bladder. It then heads to the surface to collect more air. By leaping, the sturgeon can gather enough speed quickly to swim back to the bottom of the river.

A second theory is that the Gulf sturgeon leaps as a form of communication. In the summer and fall months, it stays in the deepest parts of rivers. Biologists call these places holding areas. There, the sturgeon rests all day while hardly moving. Since it does not feed then, it conserves energy. After it leaps, it falls into the water and makes a unique splashing sound. This tells other sturgeon in the area where a good holding area is located so that they too can save energy.

🎧 A10

Directions You have 20 minutes to plan and write your response. Your response will be judged on the basis of the quality of your writing and on how well your response presents the points in the lecture and their relationship to the passage. Typically, an effective response will be 150-225 words.

Question Summarize the points made in the lecture, being sure to explain how they cast doubt on specific points made in the reading passage.

COPY CUT PASTE   Word Count : 0

A | Reading Passage

Read the following passage carefully. Try to understand what the main argument of the passage is.

Biofuels are created from organic matter such as corn and sugarcane. In recent years, scientists have been working on making biofuel by using algae. If they do so efficiently, algae biofuel could replace petroleum as the most commonly used fuel in the future.

The primary benefit of algae biofuel is that it has unlimited growth potential. Huge amounts of algae can easily be grown. All that is needed are water, sunlight, and carbon dioxide. It is estimated that fewer than 100 million acres of land would be needed to create enough algae biofuel to replace the petroleum needs of the United States. This is much less land than is currently being used to cultivate corn and sugarcane for biofuel. Algae can be grown in ponds and lakes near conversion plants, so transportation costs will be minimal. Algae could also be grown indoors in artificial ponds, thereby allowing algae farmers to control the growing conditions.

Another advantage is that algae biofuel benefits the environment. During the conversion process, carbon dioxide is extracted from the air. This helps reduce the amount of carbon dioxide which is created by the burning of fossil fuels. In addition, lipid oil comprises half of the composition of algae. This oil is what is converted to biofuel. It burns cleaner and produces more power than petroleum. So it would be both efficient and good for the environment.

Vocabulary

- [ ] **biofuel** *n* a fuel made from biomass such as corn, sugarcane, or algae
- [ ] **alga** *n* a green plant lacking roots, stems, and leaves and which grows on water
- [ ] **unlimited** *adj* having no limits; having no end
- [ ] **petroleum** *n* oil
- [ ] **cultivate** *v* to grow a plant
- [ ] **conversion** *n* a change from one form to another
- [ ] **minimal** *adj* very small; minor
- [ ] **artificial** *adj* manmade; not natural
- [ ] **extract** *v* to remove; to take out
- [ ] **lipid oil** *n* oil made from a fat, greasy substance

◢ Outlining

Write an outline of the reading passage in the space provided.

Main Point _____

Argument ❶ _____

_____

_____

Argument ❷ _____

_____

_____

◢ Paraphrasing Exercises

Read the following sentences. Then, paraphrase them. Be sure to include the key information in each sentence.

1 In recent years, scientists have been working on making biofuel by using algae. If they do so efficiently, algae biofuel could replace petroleum as the most commonly used fuel in the future.

→ _____

_____

2 It is estimated that fewer than 100 million acres of land would be needed to create enough algae biofuel to replace the petroleum needs of the United States.

→ _____

_____

3 During the conversion process, carbon dioxide is extracted from the air. This helps reduce the amount of carbon dioxide which is created by the burning of fossil fuels.

→ _____

_____

B | Listening Lecture 🎧 A11

Listen to a lecture on the topic you just read about. Be sure to take notes while you listen.

◢ Note-Taking

Main Point _____

Argument ❶ _____

_____

_____

Argument ❷ _____

_____

_____

◢ Paraphrasing Exercises

Read the following sentences. Then, paraphrase them. Be sure to include the key information in each sentence.

1 Around the world, biofuels are being used more often these days, but there are still some issues with them.

   → _____

   _____

2 We'd need an enormous number of ponds to grow enough algae to replace petroleum as a fuel source.

   → _____

   _____

3 So it's clear that despite the environmental benefits of algae biofuel, companies don't believe that it has potential as a future fuel source.

   → _____

C | Combining the Main Points

Read the following sentences from the reading passage and listening lecture. Then, combine each pair of sentences by using the given patterns.

1 **Reading** Algae could also be grown indoors in artificial ponds, thereby allowing algae farmers to control the growing conditions.

Listening Be aware that the conditions have to be just right. For example, the water must contain no bacteria and has to be maintained at a constant temperature. Don't forget about sunlight either. On cloudy days with no sunlight, there would be no algae growth at all. I suppose indoor ponds with sunlamps could be used to make algae grow. The lamps themselves would require enormous amounts of energy though.

→ **The professor mentions that** _____

_____ **. The reading passage points out that** _____

_____ **. But the professor counters by saying**

that _____

_____ **.**

2 **Reading** Another advantage is that algae biofuel benefits the environment. During the conversion process, carbon dioxide is extracted from the air. This helps reduce the amount of carbon dioxide which is created by the burning of fossil fuels.

Listening Scientists have been working with it for around three decades. But many don't think it will be eventually better than gasoline since a breakthrough hasn't been made yet. And keep in mind that right now, no companies make vehicles that can run on algae biofuel.

→ **The professor states that** _____

_____ **. She also says that** _____ **. By**

making these points, she counters the arguments about _____

_____ **in the reading passage.**

D | Completing the Essay

Complete the following sample essay which summarizes the points made in the lecture. Be sure to explain how they challenge specific claims made in the reading passage. Use the phrases to help you write your essay.

During her lecture, the professor discusses _____. While the reading passage is

positive, the professor is skeptical that _____.

The first problem with algae biofuel that the professor comments on is _____.

Like the reading passage, she believes _____

_____. However, the professor mentions that _____

_____. The reading

passage points out that _____. But the professor

counters by saying that _____

_____.

The second problem the professor focuses on is _____.

The professor states that _____

_____. She also says that _____. By

making these points, she counters the arguments about _____

_____ in the reading passage. Therefore, even though algae biofuel reduces carbon dioxide in the

atmosphere and is clean burning, it is not being used at the present time.

Modern-day nuclear power plants are safe and efficient, yet people are still concerned about meltdowns that could release radioactive material. Something that could be done to calm people's fears is to construct reactors that use thorium as fuel. Thorium is a natural element which transforms into uranium-233 when it is bombarded by neutrons. Uranium-233 is capable of producing energy for a nuclear reactor. Thorium reactors provide a number of advantages.

First, thorium itself has numerous benefits. It is three times more abundant than raw uranium ore, which is utilized to make uranium-235 and plutonium-239. They are the most common elements used in nuclear reactors nowadays. Thorium is also sixteen times more efficient at creating energy than those two elements. It decays more slowly, so it lasts longer. As a result, thorium reactors would be cheaper, so they would lower the cost of nuclear energy.

Safety is another vital factor. Thorium is safer than uranium-235 and plutonium-239. When it decays, it produces much less radioactive waste than those elements. As a result, there would be no need to construct large long-term nuclear waste storage facilities. Thorium reactors themselves are quite safe, so there would be no danger of meltdowns like the one that happened at Chernobyl in the Soviet Union in 1986. Finally, thorium's byproduct, uranium-233, is not used to make nuclear weapons. So countries with thorium reactors could not manufacture powerful weapons with their nuclear reactors.

🎧 A12

Directions You have 20 minutes to plan and write your response. Your response will be judged on the basis of the quality of your writing and on how well your response presents the points in the lecture and their relationship to the passage. Typically, an effective response will be 150-225 words.

Question Summarize the points made in the lecture, being sure to explain how they challenge specific arguments made in the reading passage.

COPY   CUT   PASTE   Word Count : 0

A | Reading Passage

Read the following passage carefully. Try to understand what the main argument of the passage is.

There are fewer than 30,000 African rhinoceroses living in the wild today. Due to poaching, the rhino is in danger of going extinct. In 2015, at least 1,300 rhinos were killed in South Africa alone while more were killed in other African countries. Due to the rhino's declining numbers, several groups are taking action to move rhinos to better-protected regions.

To do this, a rhino must first be found in the wild and then tranquilized with darts. After the animal is unconscious, the relocation team acts quickly. The members restrain the rhino and load it onto a large truck. Once the rhino is driven to its destination, it is kept inside a safe zone for two weeks. Veterinarians check the rhino to make sure it suffered no ill effects during the relocation process. Then, the animal is released into its new environment.

Most of the time, rhinos are captured in South Africa and moved to Botswana, a landlocked nation north of South Africa. The places where rhinos live in Botswana are protected much better than other areas. There is limited access to these regions by road and air. Poachers have a difficult time shipping valuable rhino horns out of Botswana, too. And Botswana has antipoaching laws tougher than those of most nations. It is therefore likely that rhinos relocated to Botswana will be able to thrive in the wild there.

Vocabulary

- **poach** *v* to hunt animals illegally
- **decline** *v* to become less in number
- **tranquilize** *v* to give medicine that will make one fall asleep
- **dart** *n* a small missile usually shot by hand or a small gun
- **unconscious** *adj* not awake
- **restrain** *v* to keep from moving
- **veterinarian** *n* an animal doctor
- **landlocked** *adj* surrounded by land; not being next to a large body of water
- **valuable** *adj* worth a lot; precious
- **thrive** *v* to do very well

◢ Outlining

Write an outline of the reading passage in the space provided.

Main Point _____

Argument ❶ _____

_____

_____

Argument ❷ _____

_____

_____

◢ Paraphrasing Exercises

Read the following sentences. Then, paraphrase them. Be sure to include the key information in each sentence.

1 In 2015, at least 1,300 rhinos were killed in South Africa alone while more were killed in other African countries.

→ _____

_____

2 Veterinarians check the rhino to make sure it suffered no ill effects during the relocation process.

→ _____

_____

3 Most of the time, rhinos are captured in South Africa and moved to Botswana, a landlocked nation north of South Africa.

→ _____

_____

B | Listening Lecture 🎧 A13

Listen to a lecture on the topic you just read about. Be sure to take notes while you listen.

◼ Note-Taking

Main Point _____

Argument ❶ _____

_____

_____

_____

Argument ❷ _____

_____

_____

_____

◼ Paraphrasing Exercises

Read the following sentences. Then, paraphrase them. Be sure to include the key information in each sentence.

1 Some conservation groups are planning to capture and ship around a hundred African rhinos from South Africa to Botswana.

    → _____

    _____

2 In the past, similar projects have seen roughly ten percent of captured rhinos get hurt, and some have even died.

    → _____

    _____

3 However, there are few people in the areas the rhinos will get shipped to, so that will make it easier for poachers to operate.

    → _____

C | Combining the Main Points

Read the following sentences from the reading passage and listening lecture. Then, combine each pair of sentences by using the given patterns.

1 **Reading** To do this, a rhino must first be found in the wild and then tranquilized with darts. After the animal is unconscious, the relocation team acts quickly. The members restrain the rhino and load it onto a large truck.

Listening The first obstacle involves the capture and shipment of the rhinos. The rhino is one of the largest and most aggressive animals in the world. It attacks both people and vehicles. To capture a rhino, you have to get close to shoot it with a dart gun. That's incredibly dangerous to the shooter.

→ **To begin with, the professor believes** _____ . **While**

the author of the reading passage writes that _____

_____ **, the professor disagrees. She remarks that** _____

_____ .

2 **Reading** Most of the time, rhinos are captured in South Africa and moved to Botswana, a landlocked nation north of South Africa. The places where rhinos live in Botswana are protected much better than other areas.

Listening Second, I'm not sure that Botswana is actually a safe haven for rhinos. Yes, it has better antipoaching laws than South Africa. However, there are few people in the areas the rhinos will get shipped to, so that will make it easier for poachers to operate. After all, there won't be many witnesses to see what they're doing.

→ **Secondly, the professor argues that** _____ .

_____ . **This is different from the reading passage. It claims that** _____

_____

_____ .

D | Completing the Essay

Complete the following sample essay which summarizes the points made in the lecture. Be sure to explain how they cast doubt on specific points made in the reading passage. Use the phrases to help you write your essay.

The professor discusses a plan to _____

_____ . She doubts that _____ . Her

opinion is opposite that of the reading passage, which _____ .

To begin with, the professor believes _____ .

While the author of the reading passage writes that _____

_____ , the professor disagrees. She remarks that _____

_____ . Then, she comments

that _____ . She states

that _____ .

Secondly, the professor argues that _____

_____ . This is different from the reading passage. It claims that _____

_____ . Although the professor agrees

about _____ , she remarks that _____

_____ . She therefore thinks that _____

_____ .

Many mammals migrate, but none travels farther than the humpback whale. It journeys an average of 5,000 kilometers from its tropical breeding grounds to its polar feeding grounds every year. During this time, it navigates very accurately. It diverts less than one degree from a straight path between its points of departure and arrival. How it does so is a mystery.

Some animals, such as birds, use the Earth's magnetic field to navigate. It is possible that the humpback whale does the same. The magnetic field does not have the same intensity all around the planet. Through experience, the whale may recognize fluctuations in the magnetic field at various points on its trip. By making slight adjustments, it may be able to use the magnetic field to travel in a straight line to its objective.

The humpback whale may also utilize the sun and stars to navigate. When it comes to the surface to breathe, it frequently uses a technique called spy-hopping. The whale rises vertically out of the water and uses its powerful tail to keep it from going back into the water for a moment. This enables the whale to observe the surrounding area. Zoologists speculate that the humpback whale may spy-hop to check the locations of the sun and stars in the sky. This then allows it to determine the path it must take to its destination.

🎧 A14

HIDE TIME 00:20:00

Directions You have 20 minutes to plan and write your response. Your response will be judged on the basis of the quality of your writing and on how well your response presents the points in the lecture and their relationship to the passage. Typically, an effective response will be 150-225 words.

Question Summarize the points made in the lecture, being sure to explain how they challenge specific arguments made in the reading passage.

COPY   CUT   PASTE   Word Count : 0

A | Reading Passage

Read the following passage carefully. Try to understand what the main argument of the passage is.

In 1876, archaeologist Heinrich Schliemann discovered a gold burial mask in a tomb in Mycenae, Greece. The mask had the face of a bearded man etched on it. Schliemann called it the Mask of Agamemnon after the Greek king who appeared in Homer's epic poem the *Iliad*. In recent years, the mask has been a source of controversy. Some scholars claim Schliemann made the mask and planted it on the site himself. There appears to be evidence supporting their assertion.

Schliemann had a poor reputation as an archaeologist. He was known to make fakes of artifacts he had discovered. There are many stories of him burying artifacts on sites and then later pretending to discover them. It is entirely possible that he did this with the Mask of Agamemnon.

Another problem concerns the mask itself. It is unlike any other masks unearthed at Greek sites. The details on the mask, which include distinctive eyes, a mustache, and a beard, are much more lifelike than those on other masks. This suggests that no ancient Greek craftsman made the mask.

A final issue is that once Schliemann discovered the mask, he swiftly closed the site and stopped digging. It was as if he had discovered what he wanted, so he had no more use for the site. This was unusual because most archaeologists would have continued digging to make more discoveries.

Vocabulary

- **archaeologist** *n* a person who studies cultures from the past
- **etch** *v* to cut or engrave with acid
- **epic poem** *n* a long poem that is often about a great hero or event
- **assertion** *n* a declaration of fact or belief about something
- **fake** *n* something that is not real or authentic
- **pretend** *v* to act like something is real when it actually is not
- **unearth** *v* to dig up from the ground
- **distinctive** *adj* having a special style or appearance
- **craftsman** *n* a skilled worker, often one able to make objects with his or her hands
- **swiftly** *adv* fast; quickly

▌ Outlining

Write an outline of the reading passage in the space provided.

Main Point _____

Argument ❶ _____

_____

Argument ❷ _____

_____

Argument ❸ _____

_____

▌ Paraphrasing Exercises

Read the following sentences. Then, paraphrase them. Be sure to include the key information in each sentence.

1 Schliemann called it the Mask of Agamemnon after the Greek king who appeared in Homer's epic poem the *Iliad*.

→ _____

_____

2 There are many stories of him burying artifacts on sites and then later pretending to discover them.

→ _____

_____

3 The details on the mask, which include distinctive eyes, a mustache, and a beard, are much more lifelike than those on other masks.

→ _____

_____

B Listening Lecture 🎧 A15

Listen to a lecture on the topic you just read about. Be sure to take notes while you listen.

▮ Note-Taking

Main Point _____

Argument ❶ _____

_____

Argument ❷ _____

_____

Argument ❸ _____

_____

▮ Paraphrasing Exercises

Read the following sentences. Then, paraphrase them. Be sure to include the key information in each sentence.

1 However, at the dig site in Mycenae, where he found the mask, the Greek authorities were watching him closely.

→ _____

_____

2 But this was a mask made for a king. Naturally, the best artisan would have made it and done an outstanding job.

→ _____

_____

3 He was more of a tomb raider. Once he found something valuable, he lost interest in a site.

→ _____

_____

C | Combining the Main Points

Read the following sentences from the reading passage and listening lecture. Then, combine each pair of sentences by using the given patterns.

1 **Reading** He was known to make fakes of artifacts he had discovered. There are many stories of him burying artifacts on sites and then later pretending to discover them.

Listening However, at the dig site in Mycenae, where he found the mask, the Greek authorities were watching him closely. He simply had no opportunity to plant any fake relics on that dig.

→ **The reading passage notes that** _____

_____ **. However, the professor says that** _____

_____ . _____

_____ .

2 **Reading** The details on the mask, which include distinctive eyes, a mustache, and a beard, are much more lifelike than those on other masks. This suggests that no ancient Greek craftsman made the mask.

Listening Some say it's too well made, so it must be a fake. But this was a mask made for a king. Naturally, the best artisan would have made it and done an outstanding job.

→ **While the reading passage says that** _____ ,

the professor points out that _____ **. She is therefore**

not surprised by its high quality.

3 **Reading** A final issue is that once Schliemann discovered the mask, he swiftly closed the site and stopped digging. It was as if he had discovered what he wanted, so he had no more use for the site.

Listening He wasn't interested in archaeological research. He was more of a, uh, a tomb raider. Once he found something valuable, he lost interest in a site. Nevertheless, just because he closed the site doesn't mean the mask isn't real.

→ **Finally, the professor acknowledges accusations that** _____

_____ **. However, she sees no problem with** _____

_____ **. She says** _____ .

D | Completing the Essay

Complete the following sample essay which summarizes the points made in the lecture. Be sure to specifically explain how they answer the problems raised in the reading passage. Use the phrases to help you write your essay.

The professor speaks about _____

_____. During her lecture, the professor explains the problems brought up in the

reading passage regarding _____ .

First, the professor discusses _____

_____. The reading passage notes that _____

_____. However, the professor says that _____

_____ . _____

_____ .

Next, the professor brings up claims that _____ . While the

reading passage says that _____ , the professor

points out that _____ . She is therefore not surprised by its

high quality. She also talks about _____

_____ .

Finally, the professor acknowledges accusations that _____

_____ . However, she sees no problem with _____

_____ . She says _____

_____ .

In the northwestern part of New Mexico, USA, lie the remains of the Chaco civilization. The Chaco people were a tribe of Native Americans. They are noted for many things, including the road system they constructed. They built more than 300 kilometers of roads ten meters wide. Many of the roads follow the cardinal points on the compass. Why they were built remains a mystery.

Some archaeologists theorize that the roads served an economic purpose. They allowed the Chaco to move trade goods to other tribes more easily. The roads permitted swift travel and let the Chaco transport large numbers of goods in various directions. The Chaco used timber to build their houses, so the roads let them easily gather and move timber from distant lands.

Another theory is that the roads were built for religious reasons. The Chaco believed in a spirit land, which people traveled to by taking a northern road. The longest of their roads was called the Great North Road and may have been their spirit road. The other roads might have also helped people travel to religious gatherings more easily.

Yet another theory is that Chaco armies used the roads. Their road system let them move strong forces of soldiers very quickly to defend their territory from invaders. In fact, the Chaco roads have been compared to the Roman system of roads, which was used for the same purpose.

A16

Directions You have 20 minutes to plan and write your response. Your response will be judged on the basis of the quality of your writing and on how well your response presents the points in the lecture and their relationship to the passage. Typically, an effective response will be 150-225 words.

Question Summarize the points made in the lecture, being sure to explain how they challenge specific points made in the reading passage.

COPY   CUT   PASTE   Word Count : 0

A | Reading Passage

Read the following passage carefully. Try to understand what the main argument of the passage is.

Sir Francis Drake was one of the greatest explorers of the Age of Exploration. He lived in the 1500s. During his lifetime, he sailed around the world and made several visits to the New World. It was on one of those visits that Drake became the first European to discover British Columbia, which is in western Canada.

Most people believe that Spanish explorer Juan Perez discovered the west coast of Canada in 1774. However, there is evidence that Drake made it there first sometime in the 1570s on his famous trip around the world. A few years ago, an English coin made during the reign of King Edward VI was found on the British Columbian coast. The coin was likely minted between 1551 and 1553. This is the third coin from that era found in British Columbia. It is highly likely that sailors on Drake's mission lost those coins while their ships were in the area.

In addition, Drake probably kept his discovery of British Columbia a secret to prevent the Spanish from learning about it. In the sixteenth century, England and Spain were constantly fighting. In fact, King Phillip II of Spain sent the Spanish Armada to try to defeat England in 1588. English and Spanish ships often fought on the oceans, too. Drake was surely worried that Spanish colonizers would flock to the area and settle there if they knew about it. For that reason, he did not announce his discovery to the world.

Vocabulary

- **explorer** *n* a person who visits new places and looks around them
- **discover** *v* to find or see something for the first time
- **evidence** *n* proof of something that happened
- **reign** *n* the time during which a king or queen rules
- **mint** *v* to make a coin
- **mission** *n* an important goal, duty, or objective
- **colonizer** *n* a person who moves to another land to start a settlement there
- **flock** *v* to go to a place in large numbers

◢ Outlining

Write an outline of the reading passage in the space provided.

Main Point   _____

Argument ❶   _____

_____

_____

Argument ❷   _____

_____

_____

◢ Paraphrasing Exercises

Read the following sentences. Then, complete the summaries below. The summaries should include the key information in the original sentences.

1 There is evidence that Drake made it there first sometime in the 1570s on his famous trip around the world.

→ _____

_____

2 A few years ago, an English coin made during the reign of King Edward VI was found on the British Columbian coast. The coin was likely minted between 1551 and 1553. This is the third coin from that era found in British Columbia.

→ _____

_____

3 Drake probably kept his discovery of British Columbia a secret to prevent the Spanish from learning about it.

→ _____

_____

B | Listening Lecture 🎧 A17

Listen to a lecture on the topic you just read about. Be sure to take notes while you listen.

▓ Note-Taking

Main Point   _____

Argument ❶   _____

 _____

 _____

 _____

Argument ❷   _____

 _____

 _____

 _____

▓ Paraphrasing Exercises

Read the following sentences. Then, complete the summaries below. The summaries should include the key information in the original sentences.

1 Recently, there has been speculation that Perez wasn't the first European to sail there. Instead, some historians claim Sir Francis Drake went there first. Well, um, there isn't enough evidence to verify this assertion.

→ _____

 _____

2 We have no way of knowing when the coins were lost.

→ _____

3 I'm sure he would have told the queen of England about his discovery, and that would have been recorded by the government. But there are no records stating that. Drake also never wrote anything about discovering a new land. Nor did any of the men on his ships say or write anything.

→ _____

 _____

C | Combining the Main Points

Read the following sentences from the reading passage and listening lecture. Then, combine each pair of sentences by using the given patterns.

1 **Reading** A few years ago, an English coin made during the reign of King Edward VI was found on the British Columbian coast. The coin was likely minted between 1551 and 1553. This is the third coin from that era found in British Columbia.

Listening Recently, some English coins from the 1500s have been found along the British Columbian coast. Some people cite that as proof Drake made it there. I find these claims absurd. We're talking about three coins. That's it. For all we know, someone engaged in fraud planted them there. There's no way to prove the coins came from Drake's voyage. I'm sure they're authentic coins, but we have no way of knowing when they were lost.

→ **While the reading passage mentions** _____

_____ **, the professor says** _____

_____ .

2 **Reading** In addition, Drake probably kept his discovery of British Columbia a secret to prevent the Spanish from learning about it.

Listening Some people also state that Drake discovered British Columbia but kept it a secret to keep the Spanish from finding out. Well, let's consider this logically. I'm sure he would have told the queen of England about his discovery, and that would have been recorded by the government. But there are no records stating that.

→ **The reading passage claims that** _____

_____ **, but the professor notes that** _____

_____ .

D | Completing the Essay

Complete the following sample essay which summarizes the points made in the lecture. Be sure to explain how they challenge specific claims made in the reading passage. Use the phrases to help you write your essay.

The professor lectures on _____ .

According to the reading passage, it was discovered by _____ .

Yet the professor disputes this argument and states that _____ discovered it.

First, the professor talks about _____

_____ . According to the reading passage, the coins are from the

_____ century. That was around the time when _____

_____ . The professor challenges this claim by

pointing out that _____ . She

also argues that _____

_____ .

Second, the professor talks about the fact that _____

_____ . The writer of the reading passage believes

Drake kept the discovery a secret to _____ .

But the professor thinks Drake would have told _____

_____ . There are no _____

though. Nobody on his crew _____ . She is sure that it

would have been very difficult to _____

_____ . She therefore believes that _____

_____ .

The Great Pyramid of Giza is one of the wonders of the ancient world. For centuries, it stood as the highest manmade structure in the world. Archaeologists estimate it took two decades to complete its construction. For years, people have wondered how the Egyptians managed to construct the pyramid. They now know that the blocks used to make it were not natural stones cut from quarries. Instead, they were high-quality limestone concrete.

Archaeologists have long believed the blocks were cut from quarries. But a careful analysis of the blocks used to make the pyramid shows there are ten standard block lengths. Essentially, all the blocks of each standard length are the same size. Carving identical blocks was impossible in ancient Egypt because the Egyptians lacked the technology to do so. The only possible explanation then is that the Egyptians were pouring concrete into molds and making blocks that way.

In 1974, a group from Stanford University visited the Great Pyramid to search for secret chambers. They used equipment that sent out electromagnetic waves. But the waves were absorbed by the blocks in the pyramid. The reason is that the blocks contained a great amount of moisture. This was curious because the pyramid is located in the middle of the desert. Quarried blocks there should have no moisture. Concrete blocks, on the other hand, retain moisture. The researchers thus accidentally proved that the interior blocks were made of concrete.

A18

Directions You have 20 minutes to plan and write your response. Your response will be judged on the basis of the quality of your writing and on how well your response presents the points in the lecture and their relationship to the passage. Typically, an effective response will be 150-225 words.

Question Summarize the points made in the lecture, being sure to explain how they cast doubt on specific points made in the reading passage.

COPY   CUT   PASTE   Word Count : 0

A | Reading Passage

Read the following passage carefully. Try to understand what the main argument of the passage is.

In the past couple of decades, the locavore movement has gained prominence. It encourages people to purchase crops grown locally on small farms. There are three major reasons why the locavore movement wants people to do this.

First, crops grown on small farms tend to taste better and have more nutrients than crops grown on industrial farms. One reason is that locally grown crops get delivered to stores quickly after being picked. They are therefore able to retain their freshness. However, crops from industrial farms must be transported long distances. Because they are no longer fresh, they lack both taste and nutritional value.

A second advantage of locally grown food is that it is environmentally friendly. Local food does not have to be transported long distances, which is unlike food from industrial farms. Thus transportation for local food uses a small amount of fuel. When food is transported hundreds or even thousands of kilometers, a tremendous amount of fuel is used. This hurts the environment.

A third and final benefit of local farms is that buying from them improves the regional economy. Food grown, sold, and consumed in the same region helps local farmers and sellers. They often reinvest money in the region, which is good for the local economy. Money paid to industrial farms leaves the region, though, and almost never returns.

Vocabulary

- **locavore** *n* a person who tries to eat food grown, raised, and produced locally
- **prominence** *n* the state of being noticeable
- **crop** *n* a plant a farmer grows
- **pick** *v* to gather fruits, vegetables, nuts, or berries from fields or trees
- **retain** *v* to keep
- **tremendous** *adj* great; incredible
- **consume** *v* to eat
- **reinvest** *v* to put profits from a prior investment back into the same business

◪ Outlining

Write an outline of the reading passage in the space provided.

Main Point _____

Argument ❶ _____

_____

Argument ❷ _____

_____

Argument ❸ _____

_____

◪ Paraphrasing Exercises

Read the following sentences. Then, complete the summaries below. The summaries should include the key information in the original sentences.

1 Crops grown on small farms tend to taste better and have more nutrients than crops grown on industrial farms. One reason is that locally grown crops get delivered to stores quickly after being picked.

→ _____

_____

2 A second advantage of locally grown food is that it is environmentally friendly. Local food does not have to be transported long distances, which is unlike food from industrial farms.

→ _____

_____

3 A third and final benefit of local farms is that buying from them improves the regional economy. Food grown, sold, and consumed in the same region helps local farmers and sellers. They often reinvest money in the region, which is good for the local economy.

→ _____

_____

B | Listening Lecture 🎧 A19

Listen to a lecture on the topic you just read about. Be sure to take notes while you listen.

◢ Note-Taking

Main Point   _____

Argument ❶   _____

  _____

Argument ❷   _____

  _____

Argument ❸   _____

  _____

◢ Paraphrasing Exercises

Read the following sentences. Then, complete the summaries below. The summaries should include the key information in the original sentences.

1 Crops grown on industrial farms taste just as good as those grown on small farms.

→ _____

2 Industrial farms are highly efficient. They can grow enormous amounts of crops on small plots of land.

→ _____

_____

3 Finally, industrial farms are located around the country. They employ large numbers of local residents.

→ _____

_____

C | Combining the Main Points

Read the following sentences from the reading passage and listening lecture. Then, combine each pair of sentences by using the given patterns.

1 **Reading** First, crops grown on small farms tend to taste better and have more nutrients than crops grown on industrial farms.

Listening You know, very much research has been done on agricultural science. As a result, crops grown on industrial farms taste just as good as those grown on small farms.

→ **Although the reading passage argues that** _____

_____ **, the professor claims that** _____

_____ .

2 **Reading** A second advantage of locally grown food is that it is environmentally friendly. Local food does not have to be transported long distances, which is unlike food from industrial farms . . . When food is transported hundreds or even thousands of kilometers, a tremendous amount of fuel is used. This hurts the environment.

Listening Industrial farms are highly efficient. They can grow enormous amounts of crops on small plots of land . . . Industrial farms are therefore helping the environment because they aren't converting forests into farmland. In fact, they're allowing some farmland to revert to forestland.

→ **According to the reading passage,** _____

_____ **, but the professor says that** _____

_____ .

3 **Reading** A third and final benefit of local farms is that buying from them improves the regional economy. Food grown, sold, and consumed in the same region helps local farmers and sellers. They often reinvest money in the region, which is good for the local economy.

Listening Finally, industrial farms are located around the country. They employ large numbers of local residents . . . So they're contributing to lots of local economies by providing employment for people.

→ **While the reading passage states that** _____

_____ **, the professor points out that** _____

_____ .

D | Completing the Essay

Complete the following sample essay which summarizes the points made in the lecture. Be sure to explain how they challenge specific claims made in the reading passage. Use the phrases to help you write your essay.

In her lecture, the professor discusses _____. She points out

some problems with the claims that are made about it in the reading passage.

First, the professor challenges a statement made in the reading passage. It argues that _____

_____

_____. The professor cites _____

to refute this claim. She notes that _____

_____.

Next, the professor counters the argument made about _____

_____. The author of the reading passage argues that

_____. The professor

agrees with this. But she points out that _____

_____. That therefore allows some land to _____, and that

helps the environment.

Last, the professor discusses _____.

While the reading passage claims that _____,

the professor states that _____

_____. They can then improve _____

_____.

The American burying beetle is a carrion beetle, so it feeds on the bodies of dead animals. It does so by finding carcasses, by burying them, and then by consuming the meat. It is the largest carrion beetle in North America. It once lived in thirty-five states in the United States. Today, however, it only lives in around four states and is considered an endangered species.

Biologists who study the American burying beetle have several theories on why its numbers have declined so much. One prominent theory blames pesticides, particularly DDT, on the beetle's disappearance. DDT was created in the 1940s and used until it was banned in the 1970s. A powerful pesticide, it caused very much harm to animals, including the American burying beetle, and the land itself.

There is additional speculation that declining populations of animals have had a negative effect on the beetle. For instance, the beetle once fed on passenger pigeons. Those birds went extinct more than 100 years ago though. The loss of this food source—as well as others—has resulted in the beetle having less food to consume.

Finally, some scientists point out the increase in artificial lighting at night. The beetle is nocturnal, so it is active at night. However, near cities, which are well lit at night, the beetle has been negatively affected. By having its biorhythm disrupted, the beetle has been reproducing less often, so its numbers have dangerously declined.

🎧 A20

Directions You have 20 minutes to plan and write your response. Your response will be judged on the basis of the quality of your writing and on how well your response presents the points in the lecture and their relationship to the passage. Typically, an effective response will be 150-225 words.

Question Summarize the points made in the lecture, being sure to explain how they cast doubt on specific points made in the reading passage.

COPY   CUT   PASTE   Word Count : 0

Part **B**

Independent Writing Task

Independent Writing Task

■ About the Question

The Independent Writing Task requires you to read a question and then to write an essay about the question. Many questions present a statement and ask you if you agree or disagree with it. You should then choose and write an essay expressing your opinion. Other questions present you with a situation and two choices. You should select one and then write your essay. Recently, some questions present you with a situation and provide you with three choices. You should select one of the three and then write your essay. You will be given 30 minutes to write your essay. Your essay should be more than 300 words. Try to make your essay between 300 and 400 words. That will be long enough to provide enough examples and short enough to give you plenty of time to proofread your essay when you finish it. The ideal essay has an introduction, a body, and a conclusion. The introduction should describe your opinion. The body should contain either two or three paragraphs that present separate points or arguments. It is more common to use three separate points or arguments than two. Be sure to provide examples to support your arguments. And the conclusion should summarize the points that you made in the body.

There are three possible writing tasks you will be presented with, but they all ask you to express your opinion about an important issue.

For the agree/disagree type, the task will be presented in the following way:

- Do you agree or disagree with the following statement?
  [*A sentence or sentences that present an issue*]
  Use specific reasons and examples to support your answer.

  cf. This question type accounts for most of the essay topics that have been asked on the TOEFL® iBT so far.

For the preference type, the task will be presented in the following way:

- Some people prefer X. Others prefer Y. Which do you prefer? Use specific reasons and examples to support your choice.

For the opinion type, the task will be presented in the following way:

- [*A sentence or sentences that state a fact*]
  In your opinion, what is one thing that should be . . . ? Use specific reasons and examples to support your answer.

◪ Sample Question

Directions   Read the question below. You have 30 minutes to plan, write, and revise your essay. Typically, an effective response will contain a minimum of 300 words.

Question   Do you agree or disagree with the following statement?

It is a good habit to take a lot of time before making important decisions.

Use specific reasons and examples to support your answer.

Sample Essay

Before I come to decisions of importance, I always consider what to do. I therefore agree with the statement and believe it is a good habit to take plenty of time before making important decisions.

I think about my choices because if I rush my decisions, I can wind up making horrible mistakes. In the past, I made decisions on the spur of the moment. For example, once, my friends called and invited me to the movies. Even though I had a history essay to submit the next day, I agreed to go with them. I wound up getting home late that night, so I could not finish my report. My teacher gave me an F, and I received a C in her class. I learned that I needed to think about my decisions in the future to avoid making similar mistakes. Now, I never rush my decisions, so my decision-making skills have greatly improved.

I also like to take my time when making decisions because that allows me to consider every possible consequence of my decisions. These results can be positive or negative. Nowadays, I sit down and consider what will happen in various scenarios. I write down the advantages and disadvantages of certain decisions. Then, after plenty of consideration, I make my final choice. I did this a while ago to determine which after-school activity I should do. I had to choose between playing basketball and learning computer programming. I thought long and hard about it. Finally, I decided to learn to program computers after I had weighed the advantages and disadvantages of each option. I am learning a lot now, so I know I made the right choice.

It is definitely a good habit to make important decisions slowly. Doing that can let me avoid mistakes, and it can allow me to consider the possible results of my actions.

Chapter 01

A | Brainstorming

Read the question below and brainstorm your ideas.

Question

Do you agree or disagree with the following statement?

People are more willing to help strangers nowadays than people were in the past.

Use specific reasons and examples to support your answer.

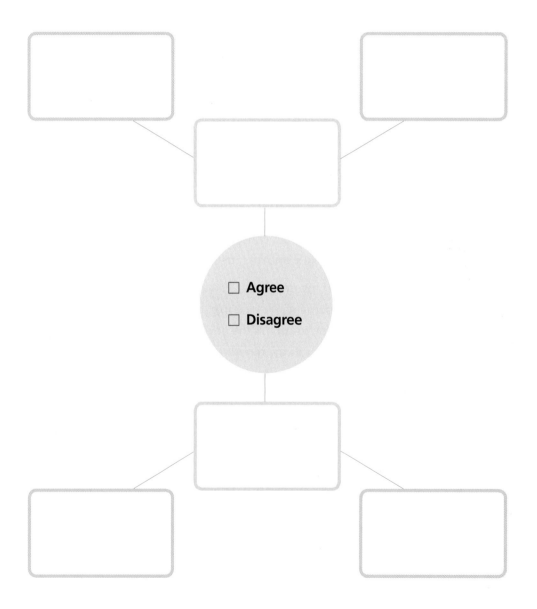

B | Outlining

Complete the following outline based on your brainstorming map.

Thesis Statement

First Supporting Idea

Topic Sentence:

Supporting Example(s):

Second Supporting Idea

Topic Sentence:

Supporting Example(s):

Conclusion

C Completing the Essay

Complete the following sample essay. Use the phrases to help you write your essay.

Agree

I agree with this statement. I strongly believe that _____

_____ . There are two main reasons that I

feel this way.

The first reason is that _____

_____

_____

_____

_____

_____

The second reason is that _____

_____

_____

_____

_____

_____

_____

People today are very willing to help strangers. _____

_____ . For these two reasons, I believe

_____

Disagree

While I know some people who help strangers, I disagree with the statement. Instead, I think

_____ . I can provide

two examples for why I feel that way.

First, _____

_____

_____

_____

_____

In addition, _____

_____

_____

_____

_____

_____

_____ . It is clear to me that

people in the past were more willing to help strangers than people in the present are.

Directions Read the question below. You have 30 minutes to plan, write, and revise your essay. Typically, an effective response will contain a minimum of 300 words.

Question Do you agree or disagree with the following statement?

It is easier for people to be educated today than it was in the past.

Use specific reasons and examples to support your answer.

| COPY | CUT | PASTE | Word Count : 0 |

A | Brainstorming

Read the question below and brainstorm your ideas.

Question

Some people believe honesty is the most important attribute for a club leader. Others prefer the club leader to be energetic. Which would you prefer? Use specific reasons and examples to support your answer.

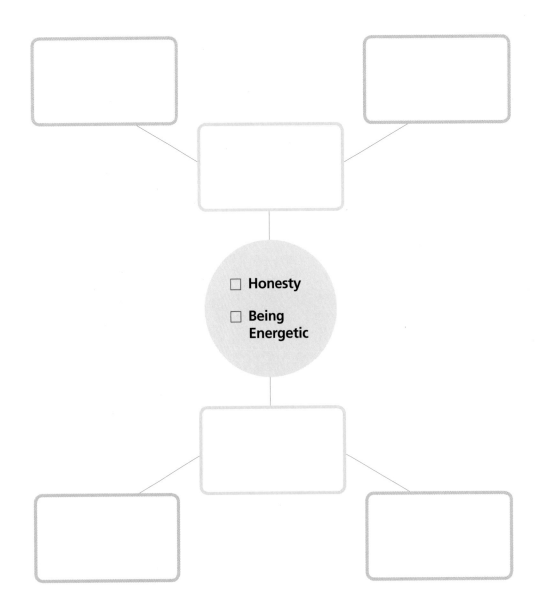

☐ **Honesty**

☐ **Being Energetic**

B | Outlining

Complete the following outline based on your brainstorming map.

Thesis Statement

First Supporting Idea

Topic Sentence:

Supporting Example(s):

Second Supporting Idea

Topic Sentence:

Supporting Example(s):

Conclusion

C | Completing the Essay

Complete the following sample essay. Use the phrases to help you write your essay.

Honesty

Being energetic is definitely an important characteristic. However, _____

_____ . Let me explain why I feel that way.

First of all, _____

_____

_____

_____

_____

_____

Another reason honesty is important is that _____

_____

_____

_____

_____

_____

It is clear to me that honesty is very important for a club leader. _____

_____

_____

Being Energetic

In my opinion, _____

_____. I believe this for two reasons.

An energetic club leader _____

_____

_____

_____

_____

_____

Another benefit of having an energetic club leader is that _____

_____

_____

_____

_____

_____

An energetic club leader can _____

_____. For

those two reasons, I prefer an energetic club leader to an honest one.

> **Directions** Read the question below. You have 30 minutes to plan, write, and revise your essay. Typically, an effective response will contain a minimum of 300 words.

Question

Some people believe that all high school students should play a sport. Others believe that high school students need to focus exclusively on their studies. Which would you prefer? Use specific reasons and examples to support your answer.

COPY   CUT   PASTE   Word Count : 0

A | Brainstorming

Read the question below and brainstorm your ideas.

Question

Do you agree or disagree with the following statement?

Young children should visit museums every year so that they can understand their country's history better.

Use specific reasons and examples to support your answer.

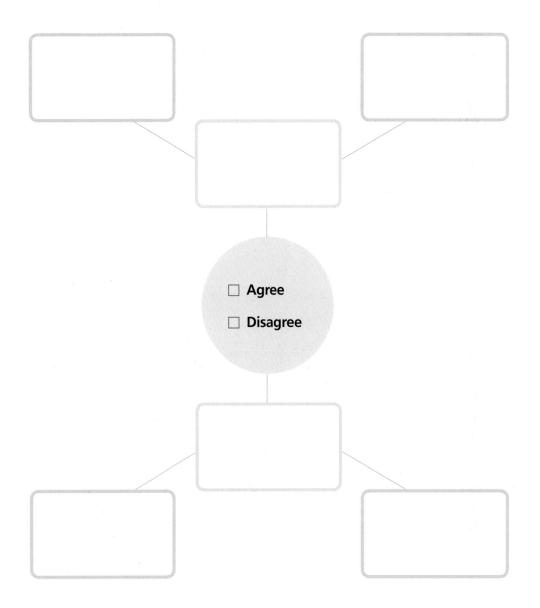

B | Outlining

Complete the following outline based on your brainstorming map.

Thesis Statement

First Supporting Idea

Topic Sentence:

Supporting Example(s):

Second Supporting Idea

Topic Sentence:

Supporting Example(s):

Conclusion

C | Completing the Essay

Complete the following sample essay. Use the phrases to help you write your essay.

Agree

I strongly agree with the statement. _____

_____

_____

To begin with, _____

_____

_____

_____

_____

_____

Another thing is that _____

_____

_____

_____

_____

_____

It is vital that young children visit museums each year. _____

_____

Disagree

While I personally enjoy visiting museums, I disagree with the statement. I do not believe that

_____ . Instead, I feel that there are better ways for them to learn.

Classrooms are much better _____

_____

_____

_____

_____

There is another reason I do not think children should visit museums to learn about their

country's history. It is that _____

_____

_____

_____

_____

_____ . For those two reasons, I disagree with the statement.

iBT Practice Test

Directions Read the question below. You have 30 minutes to plan, write, and revise your essay. Typically, an effective response will contain a minimum of 300 words.

Question Do you agree or disagree with the following statement?

The government should provide free housing to all citizens.

Use specific reasons and examples to support your answer.

COPY	CUT	PASTE	Word Count : 0

Chapter 04

A | Brainstorming

Read the question below and brainstorm your ideas.

> **Question**
>
> Some people believe students should study or play in their free time. Others think that students should help their parents with housework such as cleaning and cooking. Which activities would you prefer? Use specific reasons and examples to support your answer.

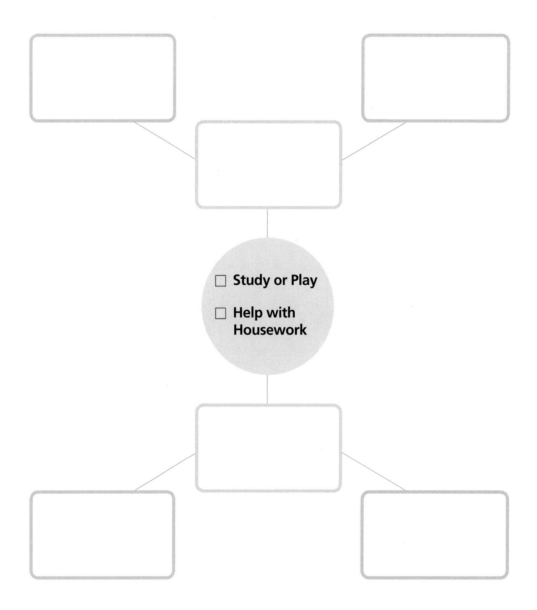

B | Outlining

Complete the following outline based on your brainstorming map.

Thesis Statement

First Supporting Idea

Topic Sentence:

Supporting Example(s):

Second Supporting Idea

Topic Sentence:

Supporting Example(s):

Conclusion

C | Completing the Essay

Complete the following sample essay. Use the phrases to help you write your essay.

Study or Play

When students have free time, I believe that they should _____. I do not

think _____.

To begin with, _____

_____

_____

_____

_____

_____

_____

Next, _____

_____

_____

_____

_____

_____

_____

During their free time, students should _____, and they

should _____. I believe those are better activities

to do when students have free time than doing housework.

Help with Housework

I understand why many people want students to study or play in their free time. I, however,

think differently. _____

_____

One reason I support doing housework is that _____

_____

_____

_____

_____

_____

Another reason I think this way is that _____

_____

_____

_____

_____

_____

When students have free time, they ought to _____. First, _____

_____. Second, _____

_____

iBT Practice Test

Question

Some people put pictures and updates on their personal lives on social media. Other people prefer to keep their lives private. Which do you prefer? Use specific reasons and examples to support your answer.

COPY   CUT   PASTE   Word Count : 0

A | Brainstorming

Read the question below and brainstorm your ideas.

Question

Do you agree or disagree with the following statement?

It is better for students between the ages of fourteen and eighteen to do many different activities than to focus on a single activity.

Use specific reasons and examples to support your answer.

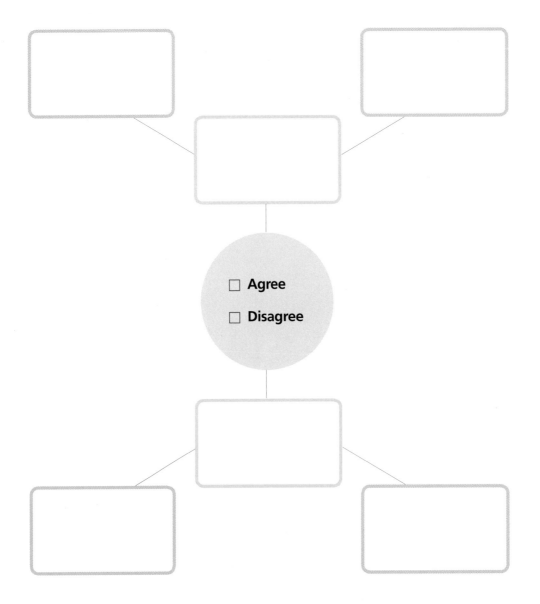

☐ **Agree**

☐ **Disagree**

B | Outlining

Complete the following outline based on your brainstorming map.

Thesis Statement

First Supporting Idea

Topic Sentence:

Supporting Example(s):

Second Supporting Idea

Topic Sentence:

Supporting Example(s):

Conclusion

C | Completing the Essay

Complete the following sample essay. Use the phrases to help you write your essay.

Agree

It is ideal for students between the ages of fourteen and eighteen to _____

_____ . I thusly agree with the statement.

One advantage of participating in various activities is that _____

_____

_____

_____

_____

_____

_____

Another advantage is that _____

_____

_____

_____

_____

_____

_____

I fully agree with the statement. The reasons are that _____

_____ , and _____

_____

Disagree

I do not believe it is smart for students between the ages of fourteen and eighteen to _____

_____ . As a matter

of fact, I believe the opposite.

If a teenager is talented at one thing, _____

_____

_____

_____

_____

_____

Another thing to consider is that _____

_____

_____

_____

_____

_____

_____

_____

_____ . Because of those two reasons, I disagree with the statement.

Directions Read the question below. You have 30 minutes to plan, write, and revise your essay. Typically, an effective response will contain a minimum of 300 words.

Question Do you agree or disagree with the following statement?

Young people should decide what they want to do for their careers when they are still in high school.

Use specific reasons and examples to support your answer.

COPY   CUT   PASTE   Word Count : 0

A | Brainstorming

Read the question below and brainstorm your ideas.

Question

The government is considering ways to protect the environment. Should it invest money in alternative energy or preserve the natural environment? Which activity would you prefer? Use specific reasons and details to support your answer.

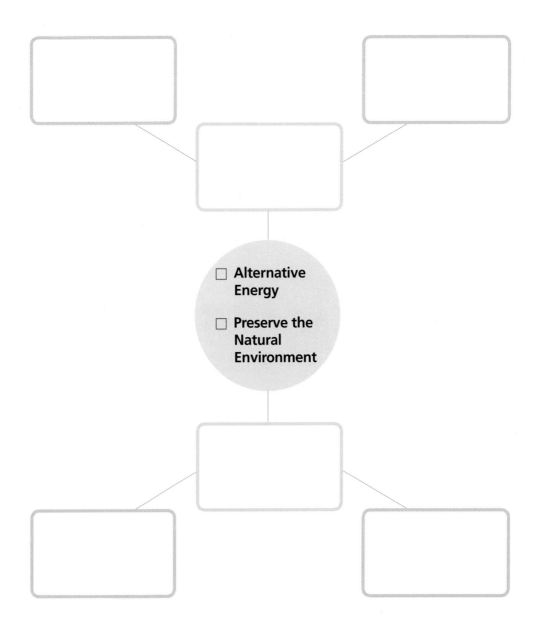

☐ Alternative Energy

☐ Preserve the Natural Environment

B | Outlining

Complete the following outline based on your brainstorming map.

Thesis Statement

First Supporting Idea

Topic Sentence:

Supporting Example(s):

Second Supporting Idea

Topic Sentence:

Supporting Example(s):

Conclusion

C | Completing the Essay

Complete the following sample essay. Use the phrases to help you write your essay.

Invest Money in Alternative Energy

I am very pleased to hear that the government is thinking about protecting the environment. Of

the two choices, it should _____.

Alternative energy includes solar, wind, geothermal, and hydroelectric power. These types of

energy are _____

_____

_____

_____

_____

_____

If people use more alternative energy, _____

_____

_____

_____

_____

_____

_____

The government needs to _____. This will _____

_____

Preserve the Natural Environment

Both of the two choices are outstanding. However, if I had to choose only one, I would select

preserving the natural environment. I think _____

_____

One thing the government could do is _____

_____

_____

_____

_____

_____

An additional benefit of preserving the natural environment is that _____

_____

_____

_____

_____

_____

I would like the government to _____. That would

_____

Directions   Read the question below. You have 30 minutes to plan, write, and revise your essay. Typically, an effective response will contain a minimum of 300 words.

Question

Some farmers are thinking about the crops they are going to grow this year. Should they focus on growing organic crops that are expensive, or should they use pesticides to mass-produce crops that are lower in price? Which would you prefer? Use specific reasons and examples to support your answer.

COPY   CUT   PASTE   Word Count : 0

A | Brainstorming

Read the question below and brainstorm your ideas.

Question

Which would you prefer, spending time with your family on the weekend or going out with your friends? Use specific reasons and examples to support your answer.

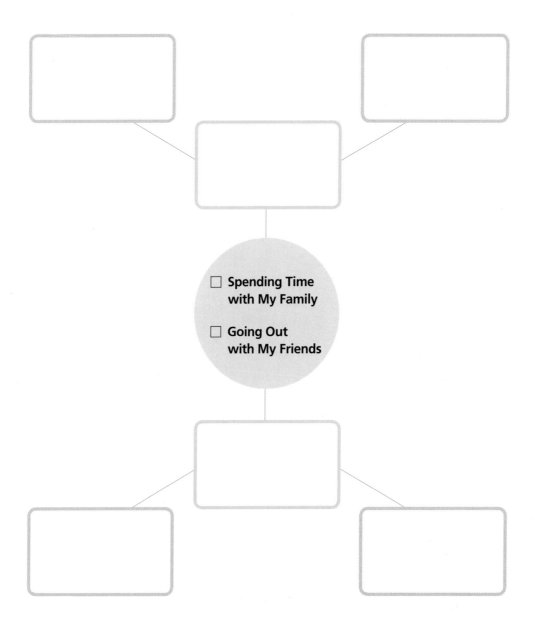

B | Outlining

Complete the following outline based on your brainstorming map.

Thesis Statement

First Supporting Idea

Topic Sentence:

Supporting Example(s):

Second Supporting Idea

Topic Sentence:

Supporting Example(s):

Conclusion

C | Completing the Essay

Complete the following sample essay. Use the phrases to help you write your essay.

Spending Time with My Family

I definitely prefer to _____ as opposed to _____

_____. There are two main reasons why I feel this way.

I definitely prefer to _____

_____

_____

_____

_____

_____

_____

The second is that _____

_____

_____

_____

_____

_____

_____

_____

_____. Thus, my choice

would be to spend time with my family on the weekend.

Going Out with My Friends

I love my family a lot and enjoy spending time with them. However, if I were able to choose, I

would _____ .

To begin with, _____

_____

_____

_____

_____

_____

Another issue is that _____

_____

_____

_____

_____

_____

_____

_____ . That is why I prefer to spend time with my friends on weekends than with my family.

Directions Read the question below. You have 30 minutes to plan, write, and revise your essay. Typically, an effective response will contain a minimum of 300 words.

Question

Which would you prefer, a job that is interesting and challenging but which provides little vacation or a job that is boring but which provides plenty of vacation? Use specific reasons and examples to support your answer.

COPY	CUT	PASTE	Word Count : 0

A | Brainstorming

Read the question below and brainstorm your ideas.

Question

Do you agree or disagree with the following statement?

It is better for young children to work in groups than to work alone.

Use specific reasons and examples to support your answer.

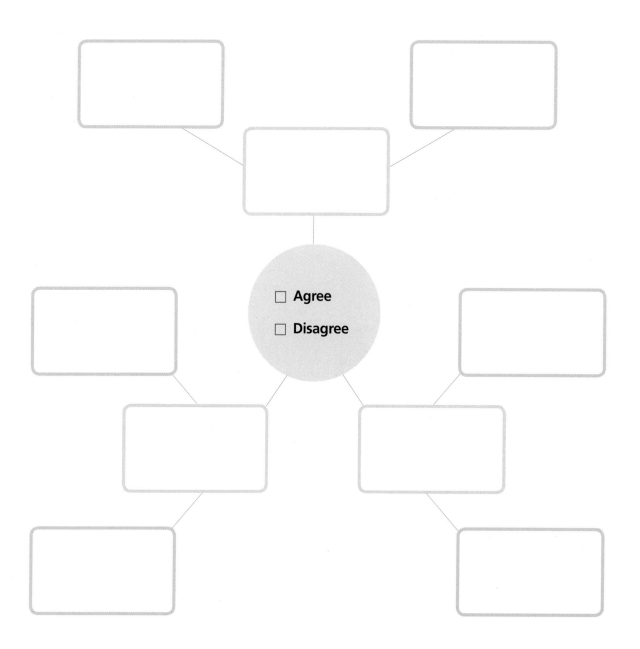

☐ **Agree**

☐ **Disagree**

B | Outlining

Complete the following outline based on your brainstorming map.

Thesis Statement

First Supporting Idea

Topic Sentence:

Supporting Example(s):

Second Supporting Idea

Topic Sentence:

Supporting Example(s):

Third Supporting Idea

Topic Sentence:

Supporting Example(s):

Conclusion

C | Completing the Essay

Complete the following sample essay. Use the phrases to help you write your essay.

Agree

When young children work, I believe they ought to do so in groups. That would be better than

working alone. I therefore agree with the statement.

By working in groups, children can _____

_____

_____

_____

_____

An additional benefit is that _____

_____

_____

_____

_____

A third advantage to working in groups is that _____

_____

_____

_____

_____

_____

_____. For those three reasons, I agree with the statement.

Disagree

I do not think it is a good idea for young children to work in groups. Thus, I disagree with the statement because it is my firm belief that young children should work by themselves.

First, _____

_____

_____

_____

Second, _____

_____

_____

_____

Third, _____

_____

_____

_____

I strongly disagree with the statement. I believe it is better for students to _____

_____. By working alone, students can _____

_____

Directions Read the question below. You have 30 minutes to plan, write, and revise your essay. Typically, an effective response will contain a minimum of 300 words.

Question Do you agree or disagree with the following statement?

You should not keep a relationship with an old friend who does something you disapprove of.

Use specific reasons and examples to support your answer.

COPY CUT PASTE   Word Count : 0

A | Brainstorming

Read the question below and brainstorm your ideas.

Question

Do you agree or disagree with the following statement?

A person's job has a greater effect on that individual's overall happiness than the person's social life does.

Use specific reasons and examples to support your answer.

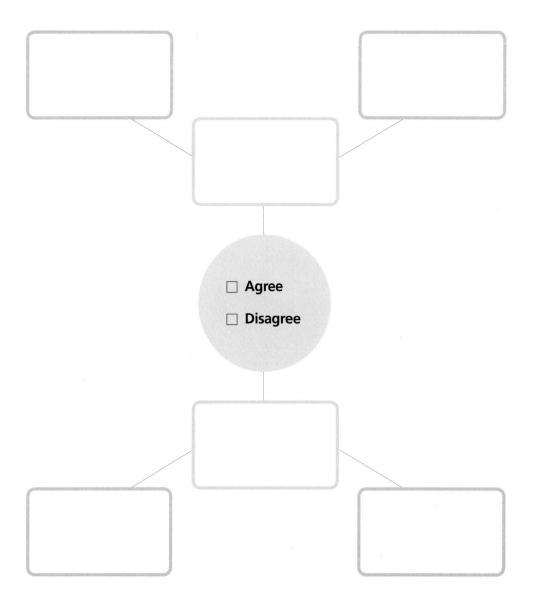

☐ **Agree**

☐ **Disagree**

B | Outlining

Complete the following outline based on your brainstorming map.

Thesis Statement

First Supporting Idea

Topic Sentence:

Supporting Example(s):

Second Supporting Idea

Topic Sentence:

Supporting Example(s):

Conclusion

C | Completing the Essay

Complete the following sample essay. Use the phrases to help you write your essay.

Agree

I fully agree with the statement. In my opinion, _____

_____.

The main reason I feel this way is that _____

_____

_____

_____

_____

_____

_____

Another reason is that _____

_____

_____

_____

_____

_____

_____

I strongly agree with the statement. _____

_____

_____

Disagree

I do not believe that _____

_____ . To be honest, I believe the opposite, so I disagree

with the statement.

For one thing, _____

_____

_____

_____

_____

_____

For another thing, _____

_____

_____

_____

_____

_____

_____ . As a result, I disagree with the

statement.

Directions Read the question below. You have 30 minutes to plan, write, and revise your essay. Typically, an effective response will contain a minimum of 300 words.

Question Do you agree or disagree that students should choose their university majors based on the kinds of jobs they can get after they graduate? Use specific reasons and examples to support your answer.

COPY CUT PASTE

Word Count : 0

A | Brainstorming

Read the question below and brainstorm your ideas.

Question

These days, it is important for many people to learn a foreign language. Some people like to study a new language in their own country. However, other people like to live in a foreign country and learn the language there.

Which do you prefer? Use reasons and examples to support your answer.

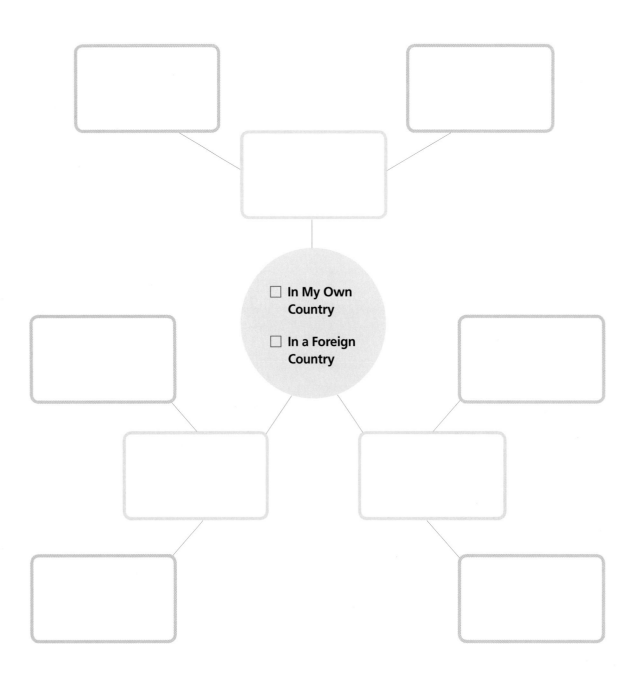

☐ **In My Own Country**

☐ **In a Foreign Country**

B | Outlining

Complete the following outline based on your brainstorming map.

Thesis Statement

First Supporting Idea

Topic Sentence:

Supporting Example(s):

Second Supporting Idea

Topic Sentence:

Supporting Example(s):

Third Supporting Idea

Topic Sentence:

Supporting Example(s):

Conclusion

C | Completing the Essay

Complete the following sample essay. Use the phrases to help you write your essay.

Study a New Language in My Own Country

Living in a foreign country and learning a new language there would be unique. But I would

prefer to _____ .

First of all, _____

_____

_____

_____

_____

Second of all, _____

_____

_____

_____

_____

Third of all, _____

_____

_____

_____

_____

I would prefer to study a foreign language in my own country. _____

_____

Learn a Language in a Foreign Country

Of the two choices, I would prefer the latter. For me, _____

_____ is the better choice.

The first reason is obvious: _____

_____

_____

_____

_____

Next, _____

_____

_____

_____

Last of all, _____

_____

_____

_____

_____

_____

I would therefore prefer to live in another country to learn a foreign language.

Directions Read the question below. You have 30 minutes to plan, write, and revise your essay. Typically, an effective response will contain a minimum of 300 words.

Question Do you agree or disagree with the following statement?

Young people were influenced more by their teachers 100 years ago than they are today.

Use specific reasons and examples to support your answer.

COPY   CUT   PASTE   Word Count : 0

Actual Test

Writing Section Directions

 Make sure your headset is on.

This section measures your ability to use writing to communicate in an academic environment. There will be two writing tasks.

For the first writing task, you will read a passage and listen to a lecture and then answer a question based on what you have read and heard. For the second writing task, you will answer a question based on your own knowledge and experience.

Now listen to the directions for the first writing task.

Writing Based on Reading and Listening

For this task, you will first have **3 minutes** to read a passage about an academic topic. You may take notes on the passage if you wish. The passage will then be removed and you will listen to a lecture about the same topic. While you listen, you may also take notes.

Then you will have **20 minutes** to write a response to a question that asks you about the relationship between the lecture you heard and the reading passage. Try to answer the question as completely as possible using information from the reading passage and the lecture. The question does not ask you to express your personal opinion. You will be able to see the reading passage again when it is time for you to write. You may use your notes to help you answer the question.

Typically, an effective response will be 150 to 225 words long. Your response will be judged on the quality of your writing and on the completeness and accuracy of the content. If you finish your response before time is up, you may click on **NEXT** to go on to the second writing task.

Now you will see the reading passage for 3 minutes. Remember it will be available to you again when you are writing. Immediately after the reading time ends, the lecture will begin, so keep your headset on until the lecture is over.

The minimum wage is the lowest hourly rate an employer can pay an employee. Many countries have instituted a minimum wage. However, in most cases, it is not high enough. The minimum wage should be raised in many places because it will provide numerous benefits.

The primary beneficiaries of the increasing of the minimum wage will be people at the bottom of the economy. Most minimum wage earners spend nearly all of their money on the necessities of life, such as housing and food. That leaves them with little cash for nonessentials. By increasing their pay, they will earn more money and have more spending power. As these individuals spend more, the demand for goods and services will increase. This, in turn, will improve a country's overall economy. Some economists believe the minimum wage in the United States should be more than $10 per hour. That would inject $22 billion into the economy and create 85,000 new jobs in three years.

Raising the minimum wage will additionally reduce poverty. A recent study showed that an increase in the minimum wage in the United States would lift one million people above the poverty line. This would make fewer people reliant on social welfare programs. The government would then be able to save billions of dollars since it would spend less on these programs. It would also get to reduce taxes, which would help tens of millions of people around the country.

Directions You have 20 minutes to plan and write your response. Your response will be judged on the basis of the quality of your writing and on how well your response presents the points in the lecture and their relationship to the passage. Typically, an effective response will be 150-225 words.

Question Summarize the points made in the lecture, being sure to explain how they challenge specific claims made in the reading passage.

| COPY | CUT | PASTE | Word Count : 0 |

The minimum wage is the lowest hourly rate an employer can pay an employee. Many countries have instituted a minimum wage. However, in most cases, it is not high enough. The minimum wage should be raised in many places because it will provide numerous benefits.

The primary beneficiaries of the increasing of the minimum wage will be people at the bottom of the economy. Most minimum wage earners spend nearly all of their money on the necessities of life, such as housing and food. That leaves them with little cash for nonessentials. By increasing their pay, they will earn more money and have more spending power. As these individuals spend more, the demand for goods and services will increase. This, in turn, will improve a country's overall economy. Some economists believe the minimum wage in the United States should be more than $10 per hour. That would inject $22 billion into the economy and create 85,000 new jobs in three years.

Raising the minimum wage will additionally reduce poverty. A recent study showed that an increase in the minimum wage in the United States would lift one million people above the poverty line. This would make fewer people reliant on social welfare programs. The government would then be able to save billions of dollars since it would spend less on these programs. It would also get to reduce taxes, which would help tens of millions of people around the country.

COPY CUT PASTE

Writing Based on Knowledge and Experience

For this task, you will write an essay in response to a question that asks you to state, explain, and support your opinion on an issue. You have **30 minutes** to write your essay.

Typically, an effective essay will contain a minimum of 300 words. Your essay will be judged on the quality of your writing. This includes the development of your ideas, the organization of the content, and the quality and accuracy of the language you used to express ideas.

Click on **CONTINUE** to go on.

COPY CUT PASTE Word Count : 0

Directions Read the question below. You have 30 minutes to plan, write, and revise your essay. Typically, an effective response will contain a minimum of 300 words.

Question

Some people believe that countries should require their citizens to vote in elections. Other people think that citizens should be allowed to choose whether they want to vote. Which do you prefer? Use specific reasons and examples to support your answer.

Authors

Michael A. Putlack

- MA in History, Tufts University, Medford, MA, USA
- Expert test developer of TOEFL, TOEIC, and TEPS
- Main author of the Darakwon *How to Master Skills for the TOEFL® iBT* series and *TOEFL® MAP* series

Stephen Poirier

- Candidate for PhD in History, University of Western Ontario, Canada
- Certificate of Professional Technical Writing, Carleton University, Canada
- Co-author of the Darakwon *How to Master Skills for the TOEFL® iBT* series and *TOEFL® MAP* series

Decoding the **TOEFL**® iBT
WRITING Intermediate ⟨ NEW TOEFL® EDITION ⟩

Publisher Chung Kyudo
Editors Kim Minju
Authors Michael A. Putlack, Stephen Poirier
Proofreader Michael A. Putlack
Designers Koo Soojung, Park Sunyoung

First published in September 2021
By Darakwon, Inc.
Darakwon Bldg., 211, Munbal-ro, Paju-si, Gyeonggi-do 10881
Republic of Korea
Tel: 82-2-736-2031 (Ext. 250)
Fax: 82-2-732-2037

ISBN 978-89-277-0883-4 14740
       978-89-277-0875-9 14740 (set)

www.darakwon.co.kr

Components Student Book / Answer Book
8 7 6 5 4 3 2   24 25 26 27 28